UNDER THE
iNfLUeNCe

UnDEr ThE iNfLUeNCe

THE SHOCKING TRUE STORY OF ANGIE TAYLOR

julia fisher

ZONDERVAN™

GRAND RAPIDS, MICHIGAN 49530 USA

ZONDERVAN™

Under the Influence
Copyright © Julia Fisher

First published in Great Britain in 1999 byHarperCollins*Publishers*

Requests for information should be addressed to:

Zondervan, *Grand Rapids, Michigan 49530*

Julia Fisher asserts the moral right to be identified as the author of this work

Scripture quotations are taken from the *Holy Bible, New International Version,* copyright © 1973, 1978, 1984 by International Bible Society. Used by permission. All rights reserved.

A catalogue record for this book is available from the British Library.

ISBN 0 551 03183 2

Printed and bound in Great Britain

02 03 04 05 06 07 08 /❖CLY/ 11 10 9 8 7 6 5

Acknowledgements

It would be true to say, and therefore not flattery, that this book would not have been completed without the help of my family and some very good friends.

My husband Norman has quietly encouraged me from the start of this project, and sacrificed many hours of my company as a result!

My sons Stuart and Neil have also shown great support, and special thanks to Neil for proofreading the manuscript whilst still recovering from typhoid. (Well, it did help to pass an afternoon!)

Jack and Joan Hywel-Davies introduced me to Angie in the first place – strange how one thing leads to another!

Clare Hordiensko and I have worked together on many a varied project, and it was to Clare that I delivered the tapes for transcription. Clare, here's the complete story!

Finally, Angie: thank you for letting me into your life. You are a courageous lady.

Foreword

When I first heard about Angie Taylor I found it hard to believe that one person could have been through so much and survived. For most people, one trauma in life is one too many. Angie has endured cruelty, abuse and addiction at a level far beyond the experience of most people and has survived to tell her story – a story that is remarkable because her life has been transformed.

When Angie first walked into the Premier studios in 1996, looking at her size (she's very small!) I marvelled that she was even considering walking from John O'Groats to Land's End. But this was to be no ordinary walk and I agreed that we would dedicate a weekly 'Angie Taylor update' programme to bring news of her progress to our listeners. To be honest, I didn't think she would have the stamina to make it. But I underestimated her spirit. Her success mirrors her steely determination, a determination that has been forged on the anvil of suffering, humiliation and loneliness. Hers is a truly remarkable story and deserves to be widely read and told.

Peter Kerridge
Managing Director
Premier Christian Radio

Introduction

If Angie Taylor had written this book herself I doubt if you would have believed it. It would be understandable to think she was guilty of gross exaggeration: how could a person endure so much and survive? So I've researched and written it for her and you can be sure that everything printed between these covers is true. I know of few people who have experienced so much hostility and lived to tell their story.

I first met Angie a couple of years ago when I interviewed her for a radio programme. She was about to embark on a walk from John O'Groats to Land's End in support of family life. All very commendable, but Angie is no upper-class do-gooder or right-wing political campaigner. Her motivation comes from her past. She has paid the high price of being an innocent child caught in the web of an unhappy family. She fell out of that into drug abuse and alcoholism. Prison then awaited her and a mental hospital became the safest place she knew. The loss of her children, prostitution, rape – her story has it all.

It became clear that Angie's story couldn't be contained in a radio interview! So the idea for a book was born.

For Angie, co-operating with me to write this book has been an excruciatingly painful experience. We sat for hours with a tape recorder as I probed and questioned, slowly extracting the sordid details of her life. This time there was no anaesthetic: Angie stopped drinking some years ago. I watched as she wept uncontrollably. There were times when I thought it would be better to stop and forget the whole idea. It just seemed too painful to unearth so many memories. But it was Angie who insisted that we persist, because she wants the world to know how her life was changed.

I compared Angie's account of her life with the notes her social workers wrote over the years. As the true story unfolded, the pain of losing her two remaining children because of her drug and alcohol addiction was worsened by the shame she felt on reading over the facts of her case.

That there's a story to tell at all is due entirely to the fact that Angie's life today isn't what it used to be. Today she's sober and in her right mind. More than that, she's using her experience to help thousands of people who thought they were useless and for whom life held no hope.

Angie understands what it's like to live without love from another human being. She understands what it's like to be homeless, hungry, longing for a drink, missing your children. She understands what it's like to wake up after a failed suicide attempt. Her story reaches to the heart of human misery and deprivation. Yet it has the answer too!

For Angie has found the answer – or rather the answer found her.

Julia Fisher

oNE

Childhood nightmares

I woke suddenly. Unfortunately I was sober. Panic hit me as I realized I was lying naked on a bed in a strange room. It had happened again. I could hear men's voices whispering. I tried to hear what they were saying, but I couldn't understand their language. They were sitting close behind me in the small, dingy room. I turned and must have startled them. One leapt across and punched me in the head, and I reeled back onto the bed. He stood over me, his arm poised ready to punch me again. I froze, petrified. His eyes darted between me and his friends. What was he going to do? Was he going to kill me?

I hated being sober: reality was too hard. I couldn't remember what had happened that night. The evening had begun as usual. I was going from pub to pub drinking as much as I could scrounge. And now here I was in a dirty, shabby little room with four Arab men I'd never seen before. I was so frightened that I wet the bed. They had raped me and now they were dressing themselves; I'd woken up too soon. I was sorry I'd woken at all. I wanted to die. The shame I felt was overwhelming. Why was I living like this?

Now the men were agitated. Was this the first time they had been with a prostitute? They were young and inexperienced. Instinctively I lay still. Why didn't they just go and leave me alone? They were in a hurry now. One of them walked out and a few minutes later the others followed. I heard the door close behind them. Finding my clothes, I struggled into them and left the room. Once outside, I recognized where I was. I'd been taken to a flat above a restaurant in Redhill, Surrey. As I stood alone on the pavement, I felt my head throbbing and my body was bruised and sore. They had treated me roughly.

I must have been so drunk that night. But now, painfully sober, I had only one thought in my mind. I did what I always did to mask the shame: I went in search of another drink. I drank and drank as quickly as I could to pass out again.

The shame drove me to drink; it was the only way I knew to bury the pain. I was imprisoned in a never-ending cycle of hopelessness. This became the pattern of my life and gradually each day became more degrading than the day before.

Today, telling my story is the hardest thing I've ever had to do, because I'm facing what I was like and I feel so ashamed of what I did. But today I'm not running off to get drunk. I've found someone who has helped me to recover. I often wonder, though, just where my life went so badly wrong.

I was born in 1951, in a village called Woodhatch on the outskirts of Reigate in Surrey, and I was named Angela after the local pub, The Angel. I'm glad I wasn't born next door to The Parson's Pig or The Slug and Lettuce. Who knows what I would have been called then!

I suppose we would have been considered a poor family. My father was a farm hand, while my mother

The Sovereign LORD will wipe away the tears from all faces; he will remove the disgrace of his people.

(Isaiah 25:8 NIV)

Contents

stayed at home and eventually had five children. I'm the oldest in the family, with two brothers and two sisters. My mother appeared a nervous person in those days, seldom venturing outside the house. But this was a thin disguise for her violent temper that would often erupt at the slightest provocation. In contrast, it was quite obvious to all who met him that my father was an aggressive, angry man.

My mother came to England from Ireland when she was just 16 years old. Her father was an alcoholic and she occasionally told me of the beatings and abuse that he had inflicted on his children. There must have been a lot of pain in that family, but she didn't talk about it much.

My father had a violent past too. Before he met my mother he had served a four-year sentence in a military prison for attempted murder. Apparently there had been a row in a pub and my father had produced a gun. He didn't actually shoot the fellow, but pistol-whipped him about the head until he was nearly dead – all because he was a German. So he was in prison during the war. I sometimes wonder if he did it because he didn't want to join the army. I just don't know the truth. He never talked about it.

I remember, when I was very young, that my dad could lose his temper in a second. This became a convenient form of discipline, because my mother used our fear of him to control us children. If we were naughty she would threaten us: 'You wait until your father comes in!' We were put in a room where we stayed huddled together until he came home. Then, sometimes several hours later, he would punish us. We were really frightened of him.

My dad's rages and violent behaviour cost him his job many a time. Before I was 11 years old we had moved house 22 times. Typically my father would have a row with someone, there would be a fight, he would get the sack, and the family would be thrown out of the tied cottage. I remember that at one place, we were there for just one night. We didn't even get unpacked. Everything was piled on the pram and the next day we were walking up the road not knowing where we were going to sleep that night.

The same thing happened on another occasion and a lady took us into her house because it was pouring with rain. That's the kind of life we had. It was very unstable and very transient. There was never much money and it was hard for my mother. I seldom saw her smile or her eyes light up; she always seemed worried and preoccupied, with unpredictable moods.

Virtually everything I know I've taught myself. In the early days, I only went to school occasionally. We moved around so much that we were never in one place long enough to settle, let alone find a school to go to. This meant I never had the opportunity to make friends of my own age: I never met anybody! For years afterwards I found it difficult to be sociable and talk to people in a relaxed way. I suppose I lacked confidence.

As I got older, school wasn't considered necessary anyway, which wasn't really a hardship because I didn't know what I was missing. I thought it was quite normal to stay at home and help with the younger children. After all, I was the eldest and I felt my mother needed me.

I did my best to help, but it wasn't easy. I used to try to anticipate her moods and compensate for her – anything to try and please her. But the truth is, I could never please her. I can't remember my mum ever hugging me or showing me any warmth or kindness. The first time I saw her do that was when Adrian, my brother, was born. There was never any love for the girls, but the boys were different. I would keep working, but it was never enough.

She didn't enjoy going out and every journey was an ordeal for her, so she rarely left the house. She was constantly pregnant, always looked ill and was permanently tired.

She was a Catholic and persuaded my father to convert to Catholicism when I was about five years old. That meant they didn't use any reliable method of birth control, so after the fifth baby was born they didn't sleep together again. This led to more pain, more bitterness and more frustration in the family. Everything was just very sad.

We lived a very isolated existence. I didn't know any other families because we lived such a rural life and went so quickly from place to place. I didn't really have anything to compare our life with – we had no radio or television, and I didn't read books or newspapers. So as far as I was concerned, I wasn't missing anything. It seemed normal to me. It was just life. I didn't realize we were a different or dysfunctional family. I just assumed everyone was the same.

We had our daily routine and everyone had their tasks to do. It was my responsibility to have my dad's slippers ready by the fire in the evening. Another of my jobs was to empty out his pockets and roll up the tobacco dust to make him more fags. I did that while he had his dinner. Looking back, I realize now how much I wanted my mum and dad to love me. They were harsh, but I really did love them and wanted to please them. I wanted them to be happy. I wanted the whole family to be peaceful, so I tried to be a step ahead of trouble in order to avoid it happening.

When I was about six years old, not that long after my father had become a Catholic, he was taken seriously ill.

At that time we were living on a farm at Turners Hill, just outside Crawley in Sussex. The area is more built up today, but it was very rural then. When we lived there, the land belonged to Lady Wainwright! One evening my father drove his tractor up to the house. I heard him coming and ran out to meet him. As he jumped down he screamed, and I watched him fall to the ground. He looked over towards me and I could see blood pouring out of his mouth. He looked so frightened and I was certainly terrified as I ran over to him. My mother heard the commotion and came rushing out to see what had happened. Between us we managed to get him into the house. An ambulance came and took him away. I just managed to kiss his toes – that was all I could see poking out of the blanket on the stretcher. They took him to Smallfields Hospital, where he stayed for months. He had two duodenal ulcers and both had burst.

Life became difficult for us then because we lived in a tied cottage. With my father unable to work, before long the farm manager wanted us out of our home. We soon found out that he was planning to evict us. Our doctor and the local Catholic priest heard about our dilemma and in a desperate, last-minute attempt to help us, one of them wrote to the Duke of Edinburgh on our behalf. The day before we were due to be evicted, our doctor and the priest barricaded themselves in the house with us.

The same day a letter arrived from the Duke of Edinburgh's office saying he had written to the local council in support of our case. Shortly after that a man from the housing department arrived to give us the keys to a council house. So we were moved to Crawley, to a proper house, a real house – and it had a loo! It had everything! No longer did we have to use a bucket at the bottom of the garden. But I was terrified of this flush loo at first, as I'd never seen one before.

Eventually my father came home from hospital, but it soon became obvious that he was too weak to return to work as a farm labourer. He took a job in a factory as a storeman instead. I was soon aware that something was different about him; his personality had changed. He became subdued. Whether it was because he'd been seriously ill or because of his new job I don't know, but it was as though a light had gone out inside him. He never enjoyed his job at the factory in the same way that he had enjoyed working on the land, but he went there every day for the rest of his life.

This change in our circumstances meant that I was able to go to school for the first time, at least for a while. I started to attend Our Lady Queen of Heavens in Langley Green, Crawley, quite regularly, and was looking forward to moving on to the secondary school when my mother decided she needed me at home again to help her. I felt bitterly disappointed. Having tasted the opportunity of education, home life seemed even more monotonous.

Despite our improved housing and my dad's generally subdued behaviour, we still lived in a climate of tension, with the threat of violence never far away. My mother's parents came over from Ireland on one occasion and lived with us for a few weeks. It was a nightmare. My grandfather was hot tempered and he and my father used to fight. One day my grandfather got drunk and before we knew it, the two men had started hitting each other. My dad knocked some of my grandfather's teeth out. I was so frightened that I grabbed my little sister and brother and ran out of the house with them. The whole thing happened so suddenly, I had no time to get properly dressed. All I could think of was getting those children to safety. Only as I ran up the road did I realize I had no knickers on! Shortly after that my grandparents returned to Ireland. They never came to stay again.

Looking back, I can see that living in this unpredictable environment turned me into an anxious child. I always felt it was my responsibility to try and keep the peace. The slightest thing could spark off a row, so I would anticipate trouble and attempt to manipulate the situation to prevent anything bad happening. I would try and bribe my sister Pam, for instance: 'I'll give you my doll, but you must be good tonight.' She'd take the doll, but she'd still be naughty, so my efforts didn't always work. My constant fear was that my mum and dad would start rowing. When they started, anything could happen. Things would get smashed.

I remember once, following a particularly violent argument, my mum went outside. There was a pile of bricks in the garden and she proceeded to break every window in the house. The noise of shattering glass seemed to go on for ages. There would be a brief pause while she stooped to pick up another brick. Then would come another ear-splitting crash. There was glass everywhere. I was screaming at her to stop. But she was cursing and shouting and took no notice of me. Then she started breaking next-door's windows. It was awful.

In stark contrast, every Sunday without fail we would walk six miles to our local Catholic church. I loved going. I loved hearing about Jesus. I learnt about him through the Stations of the Cross. I heard that he'd died for me. I didn't understand then how much he loved me. I didn't understand what real love was: I had no experience of being loved. I 'loved' my mum and dad, but they were hardly good role models.

There were two people I really admired at that time, though. I took every opportunity I could to get away from the house and visit the convent nearby. Sister Mary lived there. She was elderly and gentle and I really loved her. Some of the nuns were spiteful, but she was sweet. I wanted to be a nun because of her. I used to visit her and she would talk to me. I felt she genuinely had time for me. But one day my mother bought some grapes and I ate some of them without asking her first. She caught me and dragged me to the convent, where she told Sister Mary that I was a 'f***ing thief'. I was so ashamed. I couldn't go back there any more.

The other person I adored was my grandmother, my dad's mum. She and my grandfather lived and worked on a farm near Reigate. Sometimes we would be sent away for a week to stay there. To me it was heaven on earth. All those fields were mine and I could walk in them as I pleased and feel safe. I didn't have to do anything when I was there.

My Nan was wonderful. She was really slovenly, though. She kept budgerigars and they were all called Peter, every one of them! She kept them in cages right above the kitchen table and their mess went over everything she was cooking. She always had a cigarette in her mouth, but the ash never seemed to drop off. This used to be a source of amazement to me. How could the ash stay there like that? She would talk away, and it would still be there!

Once a week Nan made some really thick gravy and we used to have a 'slice' with our dinner. It was put in the larder to keep cool because there was no electricity in that house. They used gas lamps, and a bucket toilet that hardly ever got emptied. The place was dirty. But with Nan I could just be a child. I didn't have to do any jobs or feel responsible. I could get up in the morning and she'd just say, 'Off you go. I'll see you later, love.' She was my friend.

The person who I felt loved me most at this time was my little sister Pam. But she was so naughty. Time and time again I pleaded with her to be good for her own sake, but she didn't seem to be afraid of my mum. Instead she would challenge her. One day she said to my mother, 'If you don't leave me alone I'm going to jump out of the bedroom window.' My mother was furious with her and went for her with a strap. But Pam was too quick for her. I tried to jump in front of Pam to stop her, but she escaped and jumped out of the window, leaving her knickers hanging on the latch.

I loved her because she was so spirited and brave. But she just wouldn't conform. My mother despaired of her and complained to our doctor that she was naughty and out of control. She wasn't really – I think she was just bewildered and felt trapped in our unhappy family life.

One day, the doctor was called to the house because Pam had gone berserk and locked herself in our bedroom (shared by three of us). She had pushed some heavy furniture in front of the door and it took ages to coax her out. By the end of it Pam was a screaming wreck. The doctor gave her some medicine to calm her down and help her sleep. By the time she was 11 she was on Valium, which she took every day for years. Pam finally stopped taking Valium just a few years ago, at the age of 45. She now goes out and has a full-time job. In fact, you can't keep her in: it's wonderful!

The reason Pam became so upset was because my father's personality and behaviour towards us began to change dramatically. It started after he converted to Catholicism. At first the change was gradual, only becoming more noticeable on his discharge from hospital, when he came back to live with us in the council house in Crawley.

Maybe it was due to the fact he had been so ill and nearly died, but he seemed to undergo some sort of nervous breakdown. Then he became what I can only describe as a religious maniac. He would go to work in the factory during the day, then come home and put us through a programme of religious exercises. He made us read the Catechism and say our prayers every night. He became obsessive about it, domineering and threatening.

At around this time a visit from my Uncle PJ (Peter James), my mum's brother, suddenly made matters much worse. He had spent the previous evening with some friends and they had held a seance. Uncle PJ enthusiastically told my parents how exciting it was. He'd talked to this person and that person, and he wanted to demonstrate to them how it worked. So he promptly tore up some paper and fetched a tumbler from the kitchen.

I may have been young – I must have been about seven years old – but I remember this happening very clearly. Colin and Janice had not yet been born, but I was there with Pam and Adrian, who was only a tiny baby. I watched quietly as the adults sat huddled around the small table, their fingers barely touching the glass. I saw it moving across the table, but then we were sent off to bed.

The next night we were woken and called downstairs in the early hours of the morning. It was the beginning of a nightmare. Dad put the glass on the table. Pam and I were made to stand next to him in our nightdresses. He told us something important had happened and we were now to call him St John. The Bible had been changed and Jesus was no longer going to fight the devil at the end of history. He – my dad – was going to instead. He'd been told that he would win the battle, but only if he had the support of his family. We were then made to put our hands on the glass, and as it moved around the letters on the table it spelt out the message, 'I am Jesus.' 'Jesus' then told us that we were to do everything our father told us to do.

So one year after we had moved into the house in Crawley, our lives took another strange twist and we embarked on a period that was to last until I was a teenager.

My parents held a seance every day, sometimes more than once a day. Pam and I were so scared, but we dared not disobey. We didn't know if dad was really St John or not. I told myself he could be. I didn't see why not, because other people were saints and they had been made saints after being just normal people like my dad.

One night my dad produced a gold ring and said that this was to disperse the devil. He would walk around the house and tell us there was evil about us, circling the ring over our heads. I was frightened, but Pam was absolutely terrified. The toilet was outside (it may have been a modern flush loo, but it was still outside!) and it was a scary experience going out there in the dark. Pam and I were so frightened of going into the garden after dark that we used to keep two of my dad's tobacco tins in our bedroom to use in case we needed to go to the toilet during the night. We were genuinely afraid that the devil might get us.

Time went on, and things got progressively worse. We were called down one night to take part in another seance. It had been my birthday and my mum had bought me a second-hand pram which she had painted herself. 'Jesus' told me, through the glass on the table, that I had to give that pram away – it had to be sold. I had no choice in the matter. I couldn't say a word – I was too afraid.

Dad's behaviour became more and more bizarre. One day he put a cloth over every mirror in the house – and we had a lot of mirrors. He told Pam and me that we would go blind and something really evil would happen to him and mum if we ever looked in those mirrors. I was so frightened. What if it was true?

As for my mother, she wholeheartedly supported my father in what he was doing. She knelt down and did everything he said. These events happened in a very short space of time. Within a couple of months we were over-taken by a complete change in the family structure. My parents reversed roles. My mother changed from being in control to being submissive. Her husband had become a saint! Through the glass she was talking to people from the past and was convinced it was true. And I think that for the very first time in his whole life my father was in control. He had found a way of making us all do what he wanted us to do.

tWO

'I just want
my dad back'

It took just one night. A few people playing what they thought was an innocent party game led to years of terror. As time passed, my father's behaviour grew more and more strange and unpredictable. He began to write hymns to himself, describing how he was St John and it would no longer be Jesus fighting the devil in the last days, but him. He would save Jesus and destroy Satan!

He had two LP records of Harry Secombe singing hymns. The one he played most often was 'Onward Christian Soldiers'. As soon as Pam and I heard the sound of that music we froze with fear. We knew what was about to happen. Dad would start to duck and dive and throw himself all over the room as though he was in a boxing ring. Whilst he was doing this, my mother would kneel on the floor with her head bowed. I'm sure she believed it was all real.

Before long this kind of thing was happening almost every day, even though my dad had recently undergone major abdominal surgery for his ulcers. Pam and I were terrified that he would harm himself or us. He would fling himself about as though he was being hit, shouting that he was fighting the devil, although we couldn't see anything. In the end, exhausted and drenched in sweat, he would fall to the floor. Then my mother would get up from her kneeling position, go into the kitchen and fetch a bowl of water and some soap. Pam and I had to wash his face and his feet and dry him with our hair. If we refused we were beaten.

Sometimes he would say, 'God has put a mark on me today,' and he would tell us what it was. Then he would ask us, 'What do you see?' And we would have to repeat what he'd just told us. 'There's a cross on your back, dad,' or whatever it was for that day. We learned to listen to what we had to repeat very carefully. We dare not get a word wrong for fear of another beating.

As time progressed he did away with the glass and the letters on the table. No longer were we called only in the middle of the night. Instead, at any time of the day or night we would be ordered into 'his presence'. We would watch as he put his hands in front of his face and said, 'I'm being called.' This was our signal to kneel down at his feet. Then 'Jesus', or 'St John', or 'the devil', or the 'Angel Gabriel' would talk through him to us. He would identify who was speaking through him and we would listen as he passed on orders that we had to obey.

At this time he ran a youth club for boys, and I remember 'a voice' telling my mother that she was to go and buy some pool tables on hire purchase for the club. We had no money of our own – we couldn't possibly afford such expensive items. On another occasion I was told to sell my dolls and give my dad the money. Pam was ordered to do things as well. We had no option because it was 'Jesus', or whoever, who had commanded us. Dad had total control over us because we all believed in God and so we were frightened *not* to believe what the 'voices' said. On another occasion he told us he was going to become the first English Pope!

I didn't understand then how evil all this was: it was too subtle. I was scared, but my main concern was for Pam, who was just 9 or 10 at the time, a couple of years younger than me. My brother Adrian was still very young at this time and so wasn't really involved. But Pam cried so much and I spent most of my time comforting and protecting her. She was very afraid.

Other people started to notice my dad's erratic tendencies. He was frequently warned by his employer at the factory about his behaviour being so weird. He was once threatened with dismissal because he was caught in the loo writing hymns to himself!

This way of life continued until I was 13. As the years passed, however, I started to realize that my dad's behaviour was really a mask and I began to ask questions to myself. By this time I was enrolled in secondary school, St Wilfred's at Tilgate in Crawley, although I was very rarely there. I would have loved to have gone to school regularly. For a time I wanted to be a forensic scientist, and even now I sometimes think if only I could have gone, I would have passed exams and been successful. I don't think I'm stupid. I know I'm not educated and what I've learnt I've taught myself, but if I could learn that much just by watching and listening, then I believe I would have done well at school.

Anyway, there was a priest at St Wilfred's and on a Monday morning we were allowed to go and see him if there was something we particularly wanted to discuss. To reach his study meant climbing a back stairway (it was an old house with lots of corridors and flights of stairs). His door was always closed and after knocking we had to wait for his reply before turning the handle and entering the room.

During the two or three years I attended that school, I must have climbed those stairs about four times. I desperately wanted to knock on the door, but each time I turned round and tiptoed back down again. I wanted to tell the priest what was going on at home. I wanted to tell him about how frightened Pam was. I thought he might be able to help me. I would think about it for days, planning exactly what I was going to say, but each time I just didn't have the courage. Maybe I thought he wouldn't believe me.

I think I was becoming quite a mixed-up girl. I would say I loved Jesus, but I was also a good thief. There was never much money at home and I started to long for one or two treats, not just for myself but for my brother and sister too. My mum had a large Royal pram with a hood at each end and it had a false bottom which you could lift out and hide things in. So I used to wheel Adrian into Crawley, with Pam walking beside me, and take them into Woolworth's, where I'd steal packets of biscuits and sweets and hide them in the pram.

Then I'd push them up the road to the Catholic church and hurry in to say confession. Pam would patiently stand outside, watching Adrian in the pram while they waited for me. When I came out she would say, 'Can we eat them now?' I thought that was all right! I remember the priest said to me after one of my confessions, 'You must say four Hail Marys and four Our Fathers.' I thought that was rather harsh, so I went and picked some pears from a nearby garden to make it worthwhile!

I loved taking the children out and giving them surprises. I wanted them to have something tasty and I think I wanted something special for myself too. They seldom had any treats at home and Pam was constantly crying. I wanted to see them smile. I may have been frightened at home, but when I was out with the children I assumed an air of confidence which in turn gave me the courage to steal. I was scared in case I was caught, but I never allowed that to show on the outside. I felt I was doing them a favour, and provided I confessed to the priest, I told myself it was acceptable.

To people who didn't know me I probably appeared to be a very quiet, serious child. People of my own age would probably have found me boring. But I had such a lot of responsibility. Each week my mother would give me some money – it was never enough – and with that I would have to pay the electricity bill and shop for food. She didn't want to go out herself, so the responsibility fell on my shoulders. Everything was very serious in my life. There wasn't room for much frivolity.

Although I hadn't had the courage to knock on the priest's door and talk to him about my father, I became more convinced as each day passed that something was seriously wrong at home. I was daring to believe that his behaviour was a farce. He'd started doing even more bizarre things than ever. He made us all sit in the kitchen, several times a day, and watch him while he made a cup of tea with his eyes shut to demonstrate that he was a saint and all-knowing.

I became so suspicious that one day I swapped the tea and the sugar caddies over. It was the beginning of my release from his influence and control. I swapped them over and he made a mistake. He put sugar in the teapot and tea in the cups. I was released; I suddenly knew that it was all not true. But in that instant my dad knew his power had been broken too. The tension suddenly rose between us. A silent crisis had been reached in that moment. Here was my opportunity.

At that point I knew I had to go and talk to a priest. So I stole some money out of the housekeeping fund and caught a train to Horsham. There I went to see a priest who knew our family, Father William. He had been the parish priest at Our Lady Queen of Heaven Church at Langley Green in Crawley, then was made a canon and moved to Horsham. I didn't know him that well, but he was the person I felt drawn to go and see. I felt I could trust him.

I just knew it was up to me to do something. My sister Pam was getting more and more scared. She was on tranquillizers by this time and never went out. She was so afraid that when dad was throwing himself about she used to sit in the corner and wet herself and shake. Going to Horsham was a huge risk for me, but my resolve to be free from those years of misery and abuse outweighed any fear I was feeling.

I told the priest everything. He sat quietly and let me finish. I didn't understand his reply: he told me I would have to say confession. I was really upset. That wasn't the answer I was expecting to hear. I'd risked everything to come and see him and now he was telling me it was all my fault! I shouted at him, 'You're not fit to be a priest because my dad is really ill and my whole family is suffering, and I've come to you for help!'

Patiently he explained that I'd been a part of what had happened, I'd been involved, albeit reluctantly. Therefore I had to say confession because I needed to be free. But at that stage and with the way my mind was at the time, I felt as though he was blaming me. My mind was racing in circles of confusion. I thought I'd done the right thing in going to see him. I believed he was the only one who could help. Where had it all gone wrong? Who could end this nightmare?

Father William must have seen the desperate state I was in, because he came home with me that evening and spoke to my mother and father. I was terribly frightened. What would happen next? He persuaded my father to give him all the books and records of hymns, and the gold ring. He took all the covers off the mirrors. Then he went from room to room and sprinkled the entire house with holy water. He performed an exorcism. Then he said goodbye and left.

My father just sat there with his head in his hands, and he told my mother that if she wanted to end the marriage she had good grounds for doing so. Father William had also told her that before he left. Dad didn't say much after that, he just sat there.

I can't remember much about that evening. I was just so exhausted with the emotional turmoil of the day. Pam and I made ourselves scarce and went off to our bedroom. But later that evening I was called downstairs. I thought that was it – we did get a lot of beatings and this was bound to be worse than any I'd had before. I was really scared and Pam was upstairs being sick because she thought I was going to get killed.

My mum had recently given birth to her fourth child, Janice, and was feeling quite unwell. She called me into the sitting room and I'll never forget what she said to me: 'Well, you've got what you wanted. Now does he go or does he stay?' I was only 13, and I was being asked to decide. I looked into her eyes, but she gave nothing away. Her face was expressionless, neither angry or sad. I couldn't tell what she was thinking.

I looked across at my dad and I remember my reply very clearly. 'I just want my dad back,' I said. 'I don't want you to go, I just want you back.' He cried and held me, and I just felt so sad.

He didn't go, he stayed. What went was his control and his influence. St John was never mentioned again. That madness went as quickly as it came. It was quite uncanny: after so many years of strain and fear, an uneasy calm settled over the house. Dad, though, was immediately plunged into hopelessness and despair. He was banished from my mother's bed and he slept on the sofa in the sitting room from that day on. He went out to work in the morning, came home in the evening and would pretend to be asleep in his chair before going to bed on the sofa.

The roles had reversed once again and my mother now became the dominant person in the family. But instead of it being the end of the nightmare and a relief for us all, it was just the start of another catalogue of horrendous events.

tHREE

A craving for tenderness

The part I had played in breaking my father's hold over us left me with mixed feelings. On the one hand this 'success' encouraged me to flex my muscles of independence a little bit more, as I realized how the entire family had been controlled and manipulated by my dad's strange behaviour. But on the other hand I wavered, I felt unsure. I had become accustomed to the unpredictability of his behaviour, and there was security in the familiar, however unpleasant it could be. Now that the situation had changed, I grappled with the uncertainty of what was going to happen next. The spell had been broken, but now there was a void which had to be filled. I felt uneasy and anxious about what might happen.

The change had been so sudden. One day my dad was St John; the next day he was a broken man, his control finished, his power gone. One minute I felt responsible and guilty for having upset the status quo. The next minute I was proud of myself for having the courage to go and see that priest, bring him to the house, defy my parents and challenge their control. I felt pleased with myself for being brave enough to go through with it. It had been a huge step for me to take, to steal from the housekeeping money, catch a train to Horsham, go and see a priest I hardly knew and talk to him about what was going on in my family.

But it had destroyed my dad. He was a shadow of his former self. He was pathetic now, weak and ineffectual, at my mother's mercy. I felt heartbroken for my father. He cried so much; it was very sad. I was torn between submission and rebellion. I was silently screaming for help but I didn't know where to turn, who would listen, who could help.

The situation in our family had changed, but it wasn't any better. I argued the case out with myself, the debate going round and round in my head. My emotions were on a roller coaster. Deep down in my heart I knew I'd done the right thing. I told myself I'd done it for the children's sake. Everything I'd done, I'd done for them. It was the consequences of what I'd done that I was unsure about. A sort of power vacuum had developed between my parents. I could sense it and I was watching and waiting, anticipating what might happen next. I felt nervous all the time, and even more protective of my sister Pam.

Outwardly things stayed the same. I continued to make the meals and do all the shopping. My mum was ill a lot of the time, and now she had been shown that her husband was not a saint after all, she was having to come to terms with that reality too. He was clearly going through a mental breakdown, and the role that she had become accustomed to him playing, had encouraged and come to enjoy, had suddenly been taken away. The effect of this loss on my mum showed itself in some strange ways.

On one occasion, when she was heavily pregnant with Colin, her fifth baby, and quite ill, she dragged the kitchen table into the back garden and put it next to the hedge which divided our garden from our neighbour's. On top of the table she placed a kitchen chair, then climbed up onto the chair and started cutting the hedge. Inevitably our neighbour was soon out asking her why she was cutting the hedge in her condition. Didn't she have a husband who should be doing that for her? What was he thinking of, sitting back doing nothing, watching her do all the work when she was so unwell and had so many children to look after?

I suppose that was her way of getting the sympathy she so desperately craved, but I found her method of publicly punishing my dad humiliating.

Despite my nervousness and misgivings, I was slowly but surely becoming more independent. I had shown myself that the control my parents had exercised over me was false and I was determined to continue my fight for freedom. Aged 14, I was starting to change. I found life at home increasingly restrictive and my parents' demands intolerable and often demeaning.

Physically I was no longer a girl, I was becoming a young woman capable of attracting men and holding their attention. All my life I'd been used and abused and I was fed up with it. I wanted to be treated with a bit of respect and kindness. Tenderness was something I'd never experienced, but I guess that's what I was longing for.

I was going out with a boy but I didn't like him – in fact I hated him because my dad had chosen him for me. I was expected to go along and help my dad with his youth club for young boys, and this 'boyfriend' came from there. It may sound horrible now, but I still think the same way about that boy. He was boss-eyed and had a pigeon chest and he kept trying to touch me. I didn't want anything to do with him.

He must have grown tired of me because he came into the youth club one night and complained about me, to my father, in front of all the other boys. 'She won't let me touch her!' he yelled. I didn't know what to do. But my father did. In front of all of those teenagers, my dad knocked me from one end of the hall to the other. He just hit me and hit me and hit me, and then he said, 'Get out there and f***ing kiss him!'

Inside I fumed with anger. How dare he humiliate me like this? Was I that worthless to him? Why didn't he love me and treat me properly? Why wasn't he proud of me? I was his eldest daughter. Didn't he realize I had feelings? In the depths of my being I was crying, craving for some of the tenderness I'd never known.

You would never have guessed my real feelings from the expression on my face. I knew from bitter experience how to maintain a passive exterior; I'd learnt how to survive the hard way. When abuse is your constant companion there are things you learn in order to lessen the inevitable damage. You learn how to minimize the attack, and facial expressions are a powerful deterrent. I knew, better than any animal, that a submissive expression signals the end of the contest – for the time being at any rate.

At around this time, my mother was in Crawley Hospital having just given birth to Colin, and I was at home looking after the kids. I had just started my periods and was feeling unwell, preoccupied and tired. I went to the hospital to visit her and see the new baby. She'd told me to bring in some baby clothes for Colin to wear as she was due to bring him home the next day.

Whether it was because it was so warm in the hospital I don't know, but as I walked into the ward my head started to swim and I felt giddy. I could see my mother and I fixed my gaze on her and tried to keep walking towards her, but suddenly everything went blurred and I passed out. I used to faint a lot as a child – I think I was anaemic.

As I came round, a nurse was by my side talking to me and gently stroking my face. She lifted me up and helped me over to my mother's bed. I felt sick, my legs were shaking and I just wanted to sink down into a chair. But in front of everyone my mum hit me. All she could say was, 'So you want all the f***ing attention do you, do you now? Well have this, cop this!' She just went mad because everyone had turned to look at me instead of her. At that moment I hated her.

I understand now that it wasn't her fault. She wasn't living a life, she was living an existence, destroying everybody she should have loved just so she could get a few minutes of sympathy. I'm not describing someone who was merely selfish here. I'm trying to show you my mum as the insecure, deeply unhappy person that she was. She'd had a rotten upbringing. She'd never been properly loved or appreciated. Her father was an alcoholic who had abused his children. He'd abused her until she felt compelled to run away. And now she had five children of her own and she couldn't cope. Yet her loyalty to her husband was unquestionable.

She worked so hard, she wore herself out. In so many ways I did admire her. In between severe bouts of agoraphobia, she had several small jobs to make ends meet. She worked in a kitchen and one day cut herself very badly. She was carving some meat when the knife slipped, giving her a severe cut between her thumb and forefinger. She didn't have time to go to the hospital to have it properly cared for. Instead she bandaged it up herself, and finished her work in time to be home for her own family. It was a deep wound and should have been stitched. It became infected and she developed tetanus.

She was really very ill. I can remember visiting her in hospital and for a while we were left wondering whether or not she would survive. But she pulled through and before long returned to her jobs. Thanks to my mum, we were never in debt, although money was always short. She was fastidious about making sure the bills were paid on time, and I admired her for that.

But this latest incident at the maternity hospital reinforced my desire for escape. I started to plan how I could get away from the house and find my own way in the world. I was just a young teenager, but I felt grown up and quite capable of looking after myself. I was no longer the little girl who had tried so hard to please and keep the peace. I felt spurned, taken for granted and unwanted. I started to rebel openly.

At about the same time I decided there was no God. How could there be? If there was a God, he would have heard my prayers by now and come and rescued me. My whole life had been controlled by my parents. I'd never been allowed to go out by myself and make my own friends. Even my boyfriend had been chosen for me and I hated him too. When we walked up the road I would spit at him and bark orders. 'Walk behind me!' I'd say. I really loathed him and didn't want him near me.

I was starting to behave like a caged animal looking for the merest chance of escape. I wanted to run away and never see any of them again.

When I was 16 I took a job at Mallory Batteries at Manor Royal, an industrial estate in Crawley. I had a friend there called Christine. We often used to talk about what we'd like to do, how we'd like to find some work that took us away from our home area.

We started to make some enquiries and before long we were offered a job working for the Spina Bifida Association. It involved travelling all over the country selling the equivalent of a lottery ticket to raise money for the charity. The idea was that we would spend a certain amount of time in each town and the Association would provide us with accommodation. At 16 this felt like the chance of a lifetime!

But when I went home and told my parents what Christine and I were proposing to do, they were livid and beat me up. How dare I think about leaving? My dad held me down while my mum hit me and pulled out great chunks of my hair. My nose was bleeding and my face was cut.

That night I left home. I'd been offered a position that gave me a passport to freedom. I had to accept it. So I went to stay with Christine and her parents for a couple of nights, then we left for Brighton, settled ourselves in a flat and started to work at our new job.

A few days later, two policemen called at our flat. Apparently my mother had reported me missing to the police, with the suggestion that I might be living on 'immoral earnings'. I was taken to the police station in Brighton and questioned to prove that I wasn't living by prostitution.

We were left alone for a while after that, and for a few months life settled down. Christine and I were enjoying our work and being very successful. Then a telegram arrived from my mother to say my sister Janice was dying. Apparently she was pining for me and was refusing to eat. I was missing my brothers and sisters anyway, so to hear that Janice was ill filled me with remorse. She clearly needed me. I left my job and flat in Brighton and returned home.

I tried to pick up more or less where I'd left off with the kids, but of course I'd changed – I was used to my independence now. It wasn't long before I felt as though I'd been tricked into going home. Janice wasn't all that ill and soon recovered. I wanted to leave again, but of course by then I'd lost my job in Brighton.

I felt resentful and started to lead a promiscuous life, with several boyfriends at the same time. I went out whenever I wanted to and I slept with them all. They only had to show a little kindness or say they liked me and I'd fall in love. If they put their arms round me I didn't want them to let go. I'd do anything to please them.

I thought I knew what I wanted. I wanted my own children and I wanted to be away from that house. I wanted to be free. But at the same time I felt very responsible for my brothers and sisters. What was I to do?

I started to drink – not excessively, but I enjoyed going to pubs and parties. I was mixing with people who were having fun; they were friendly and they accepted me; they even liked me! It was as though I'd moved into a different world, a world of colour. I was so used to a grey existence and now I'd found something exciting and vibrant. I became even more rebellious at home and my parents couldn't control me. I came and went as I pleased.

Having lived such an isolated existence, I didn't have a lot of confidence. I didn't have any history or experience on which to base my life, because I hadn't been in the outside world very much. I was afraid to say too much about myself to any of my new friends for fear of sounding boring. Who, I thought, wanted to hear about my family? I didn't want to talk about them. I must have appeared quite pensive and reserved.

I listened and I watched what other people were doing, and soon I started to be attracted to a group of people who clearly had their own strong group identity. I wanted to have some kind of identity too, to belong somewhere I was welcome.

One day I glanced out of the window from the office at Boots, the chemists, where I was working. I looked down into Queens Square in Crawley. A group of hippies were there, sitting on their Afghan rugs. They had long hair and were smoking joints and playing music. I thought: I'm going to become a hippie. I was immediately attracted to them, I remember it so clearly. They looked relaxed and peaceful, and I wanted to be like that too.

I quickly worked out that I could easily transform myself to look like them. Clothes had become very important to me because I hadn't had many when I was young. I was a Mod, and very fashion conscious. But at that moment I decided I was going to change all that. I took my time, wanting to get it right. I was planning my next escape and this time I wasn't going to get caught and have to come back home again.

So I bought some long skirts and gradually turned myself into a hippie. I found out which pubs the hippies went to and started going along just to be with them. At first I stayed on the edge of the group, watching, listening, learning, wanting desperately to please them so that I could be identified as one of them. I wanted to belong. I knew the closer I could get to them, the more their lifestyle would rub off onto me and I could be absorbed into the group.

I was about 17 by then. I thought my own family didn't want me. I told myself they wouldn't miss me. All I wanted was to join another family, a group of people who would like me and accept me and call me one of them. Gradually I got to know one or two of the group.

My plans were temporarily held up when I was involved in a serious car accident. I hadn't been wearing a seatbelt. My face was very badly cut and I was extremely shaken. It took me several months to recover, but during this time I changed my job to another chemist, and never gave up on my plan to turn myself into a hippie.

I would have 'escaped' sooner, but my mother was ill again. She had a nervous breakdown and was suffering from agoraphobia. She would wait outside the shop where I was working, with the youngest children sitting in the pram. When I left in the evening she would rush up to me and run off, leaving me to take the kids home and give them their tea. I went along with it, but this time I wasn't going to get caught for ever. I had a goal. I was determined to break free and join the hippies.

A year passed since the start of my plan. My transformation was complete. I had changed myself into looking like a hippie; my face had recovered sufficiently from the injuries of the car crash, and I was ready to make my next move. I didn't have to wait long.

One night I went into a pub and saw a young man standing by the bar. I watched him for a long time before saying to my friend, 'I'm going to marry him.' He was everything I wanted *and* he had long hair! He would provide me with the way into the hippie people.

My patience was rewarded: I was married by the time I was 18.

fOUR

Shattered dreams

The minute I saw him I knew he was the man I was going to marry. I sat down at a table in the corner of the pub where I could watch him from a safe distance. The place was full of people, hippies mainly, moving between groups, talking together, content in each other's company. They all appeared friendly, warm and relaxed. My friend went to the bar to order our drinks. Alone, I sat and stared at this man, watching his every gesture. He looked so gentle, so at ease with himself.

I made up my mind. It was time to let him know I was watching him. I wanted him to leave the group he was with and come over to where I was sitting and talk to me. I didn't have the confidence to go and join the crowd he was mixing with – there were too many people and I didn't know any of them. I had transformed myself into a hippie; I was wearing all the right clothes. I just needed to find a way into the group and be accepted by them, become one of them.

Up to that moment I was a hippie in isolation – what a contradiction! But I believed I had found the man who was going to come to me and, walking beside me, take me over the bridge, out of my lonely, grey existence into his world of colour, peace and happiness. Nothing else mattered.

I felt a surge of excitement twinged with a sense of danger. Was this really what I wanted? Were these people as peaceful as they looked? If I joined them, would I be happy, happier than I'd ever been in my life? Would they give me the love and sense of belonging I yearned for? I still had time to change my mind. I could walk out of that pub and forget the whole idea. I argued the case in my mind and finally convinced myself I had nothing to lose. I had made up my mind: he was the man I was going to marry.

It wasn't long before he noticed I was staring at him. My plan was beginning to work. He moved away from the people he was with and started to walk casually towards me. Our eyes met. I knew that if I looked away he would turn round and walk off, pretend he was going to talk to somebody else. He knew enough people in the pub to talk to almost anyone.

I fixed my gaze. I was committed. By now he knew I wanted to meet him and I succeeded in drawing him across the room to the table where I was sitting. We talked, and within three months Dick Boorer had asked me to marry him.

He was a roadie with a group called The Mysterious Babies, who later changed their name to Train. They played heavy-metal music, rock and blues. Meeting Dick changed my life. Suddenly I was part of a group of long-haired singers! They did quite well. They made a couple of records and you could even hear them on the radio. They did a concert tour around the country. I had never had such excitement. I went to their parties and festivals. I went with them when they played at the Lyceum. I was 'with' the band, I was one of the 'in' people. I had arrived!

At last our wedding day arrived. We were married in Horsham Registry Office on 26 January 1969. I was just 18. Dick was 19. The band came to the wedding. My mum and dad were there with my brothers and sisters. Dick's father came; his mother had died a few years previously. Unfortunately, Dick arrived at the registry office covered in blood. A stone had gone through the windscreen of the car he was travelling in and hit him in the face!

I remember going to bed on my wedding night believing I was never going to be frightened or lonely again. We lived with Dick's father for a short time before moving into a one-bedroom flat in Brixton. We both had work and, although there was never a lot of money, for a time I thought life was great. Everything was going fine. We had our own place. I was free and enjoying this really unusual lifestyle. I didn't wear shoes for two years because I was a *real* hippie, a hardened hippie!

The Mysterious Babies didn't last. The band split up not long after we were married. Dick found another job as a salesman based in Cambridgeshire. By now I was expecting our second baby (I had a miscarriage and lost our first child shortly after we were married) and we decided to have a bungalow built in March, in Cambridgeshire. While Dick was working in Cambridgeshire during the week I didn't want to stay in Brixton on my own, so I decided to move back home with my mother. I stayed there for several months, although it was a move I was later to regret.

My son Chay was born on 7 March 1971. I felt I had to go out to work so that Chay could be properly provided for, and so my mother took an increasingly influential role in looking after him for me during the day.

Dick was unhappy living away from me and eventually lost his job in Cambridgeshire. He returned to London, found a job in a factory working as a lathe turner, and we moved into a house in Choumert Road in Peckham. Dick had kept in touch with his hippie friends and it wasn't long before our house became the place to visit and spend hour after hour smoking dope. I hated the stuff because it made me very paranoid and unable to talk.

Dick was very lovable and gentle, but he was just drifting from one joint, one trip to the next. Any money he had he spent on dope or music. I couldn't complain: I'd opted to be in on that scene. That was exactly what I'd chosen and that was exactly what I got. I began to see the reality of the lifestyle I'd married into: I had to share Dick with countless other people. I began to feel as though I wasn't married to him alone – rather I was married to the group he mixed with.

Dick and I had five children altogether. I had a late miscarriage and then Chay was born. Then I had another late miscarriage, virtually a still birth because it happened towards the end of the pregnancy. I fell pregnant again with Bonita when we were living in Peckham.

I suppose our relationship started to fall apart not long after we were married – certainly by the time Chay was born. Once we had Bonita as well, Dick just couldn't handle the responsibility. Soon I discovered he was being unfaithful to me. He'd been to bed with a couple of my friends and eventually he did leave me for someone else.

I went into hospital when Bonita was born on 19 May 1973, but Dick didn't come to see me. The first time he saw his daughter was when he came to take us home. He arrived at the hospital with his friends. I climbed into the van and we drove home. They all came in and smoked a joint while I just carried on as if nothing had happened.

They seemed oblivious to the fact that I'd just had a baby – they weren't even interested. I started to feel alone and frightened. That was the beginning of my agoraphobia.

One day sometime after that I was at home alone with the children. Bonita was still a little baby, Chay was just a toddler, and I was pregnant again. All of a sudden I had what I now know was a panic attack, a terrible feeling of being rooted to the spot. I felt I was going to drop dead. I couldn't breathe, my tongue was dry, my heart was racing. I ran out of the house and then ran back in. I just didn't know what to do. I spent the next few days in bed because I was too scared to get up. Eventually I went to the doctor and he referred me to the Royal Maudsley, a psychiatric hospital. All they did was to prescribe me tranquillizers and discharge me.

We moved back to live with Dick's father for a while because I wanted to get out of Peckham. We were in arrears paying the rent, the house was in a rough area and I didn't feel safe living there. The property was crawling with mice – we could hear them. I had the house looking clean and tidy on the surface, but when we lifted some floorboards and discovered a thick layer of mice skeletons (the result of a previous gassing), I could stand it no longer. It was an awful sight.

I was permanently scared and reasoned that if we moved away it might do us all good. Dick resented my mother visiting so often and being so involved with the children, which in turn provoked a lot of friction between us. I thought she was coming to help me and argued with Dick about it, which I suppose made him feel rejected.

I felt increasingly uncertain. Nothing was going according to plan. What had happened to all my fine dreams of security and happiness? All my hopes were crumbling around my ears. I didn't know what was going to happen next. I felt I'd got myself into a mess and I didn't know what to do or who to turn to. And I didn't want the baby I was expecting. Secretly I did everything I could to get rid of him. I climbed vigorously up and down stairs. I lifted heavy things. I knew that if I had another baby I wouldn't be able to cope.

Erin was born while we were living with my father-in-law. He had Down's syndrome and only lived a very short time. I held him for a few minutes and he cried just before he died. Then the midwife took him from me and put him in a stainless-steel bowl while she went to call for a doctor. Alone for a few minutes, I couldn't take my eyes off him. From where I was lying all I could see were his legs hanging over the side of the dish and his black hair. Dick didn't come and see me. He never met his son.

I didn't come to terms with the guilt I felt about Erin until years later. I just bottled it all up. Nobody else seemed to care. I never admitted I hadn't wanted him, either. I went back to my father-in-law's house and carried on as usual because I thought it was the casual, cool thing to do. Instead of grieving like I really should have done, I just didn't talk about it with anybody.

Meanwhile, Dick and his father had been aggravating each other. They were such different personalities. Dick's father was a military man and found his son's casual attitude to life extremely irritating. He thought Dick was a layabout. Sometimes he got so angry he would come up the stairs to our bedroom and kick Dick in the back as he lay in bed because he felt he should be up and working, supporting his family.

The matter soon resolved itself, because in 1974, within a few days of Erin being born, Dick left me. He told me I was a mess and unattractive, and he resented me spending the money I earned on the children. While I'd been in hospital having Erin, he'd been having an affair with another woman called Sandra, who had a little boy – and attractive underwear, Dick said. So he was leaving me and going to live with them.

The day Dick came to collect his belongings, he brought Sandra and her son with him. They sat in the car waiting for Dick while he came in to pack his bags. Chay idolized his dad and wanted to go with him. Unmoved by his own son's pleadings, Dick just shut the door behind him and left. Chay stood on a chair and looked out of the dining room window, sobbing inconsolably because his daddy had gone away with another little boy. He cried and I cried, and I suppose I wasn't much use to my son either. The agoraphobia had got so bad by that stage that I couldn't even leave the house to take the children out for a walk.

So I was left alone in the house with my father-in-law. I knew I wouldn't be able to stay there indefinitely. Dick's father couldn't understand what was the matter with me. Surely I could just 'pull myself together'? He often went out in the evenings to meet his friends and I'd find myself alone in the house after the children had gone to bed. That's when I started to drink. It began with just one glass of sherry. Then two or three. I found it just took the edge off the anxiety I was feeling. I was trying to come to terms with the agoraphobia, but instead it was getting worse and worse.

I had to go to court for a legal separation because I wanted custody of the children. At least this was easy. Dick wrote a letter to the court saying he didn't ever want to see them again (he didn't want the financial responsibility), so he wouldn't be contesting the case. However, the court ordered that I had to leave his father's house, because Dick had a right to bring his new girlfriend and child home. After all, it was his family home.

With nowhere else to go, the children and I spent the months that followed living in bed-and-breakfast accommodation. We had to clear our room every morning after breakfast and carry all our belongings around with us until we could go back in the evening. It was a nomadic, insecure existence. I spent most of my time sitting in the council offices trying to get something better for us.

I started having a glass of sherry in the morning. I thought I'd found a friend and I believed it was easing the agoraphobia, but I hadn't found a friend at all: it was controlling me. It wasn't long before I was drinking a bottle of sherry a day. I used to keep some in a medicine bottle in my pocket. I'd hold it all the time I was out, and if a panic attack happened I'd tell myself it was all right because I had the sherry there and that would help me get home.

The drink had started to take over my life. It actually happened alarmingly quickly. I was on a downward spiral heading for doom and I didn't have any friends of my own to turn to for help. The only people I knew were Dick's friends because I had joined his crowd, and now they were with him. My mind often turned to thoughts of Erin. His death seemed to haunt me, but I still didn't talk about it to anybody. The drinking got worse. With my mind in such turmoil, I tried to care for my two children as best I could.

After living for some months in the bed-and-breakfast accommodation, I gratefully accepted a job with a man in Redhill to work as his housekeeper and child minder. His wife had left him with a young son. He needed some help with the cleaning, and in return he let me and the children share a room in his house. The situation quickly turned sour. He was a strange man, and it wasn't long before he was putting pressure on me to sleep with him. I wouldn't give him what he wanted, so he made life difficult for me and at times I found his behaviour threatening.

It was a struggle to keep going, and the agoraphobia just seemed to get worse and worse. After another visit to the council offices, when I pleaded with them to find me somewhere safe to live, we were placed in a guesthouse for homeless families in Horley. We stayed there for a short time before being given our own flat in Timperley Gardens, Redhill.

At last, I thought, here was an opportunity to settle down and enjoy some peace and normality with Chay and Bonita. But I was about to meet somebody who would change the course of my life again. I met him walking into Redhill one morning. I didn't know the area all that well and was trying to find a shop, so I asked a couple of men for directions. One of them was particularly helpful and friendly. He offered to walk to the shop with me, and that's how I met Bob. We continued to see each other and before long I realized I'd fallen in love with him. He was quite different to any other man I'd known.

fIVE

The drugs trap

Twelve months had passed since Dick had left me alone with the children. It had been far from easy. Living in bed-and-breakfast accommodation and moving from place to place had taken its toll on me. I don't know how much longer I could have survived living like that, coping with agoraphobia as well.

I was drinking quite heavily by the end of the year. It was the only way I could cope with each day. But the moment I met Bob I stopped drinking. I didn't need it. I put down one crutch and picked up another. I put down the drink and picked up Bob.

It wasn't long before he came to live with us and for a while I was ecstatically happy. I began to relax and feel better. The fear that had gripped me in a vice started to subside. Bob was kind and loving towards Chay and Bonita; they had a dad again and we quickly became a close family unit.

Some time later Bob told me there was something I needed to know: he was a registered heroin addict. But he assured me that he hadn't taken any heroin since meeting me. That proved it for me – we were just right for each other! I'd stopped drinking and he'd stopped taking heroin.

I believed him until he started to disappear for long periods of time. Slowly and reluctantly I came face to face with the awful realization that I had probably made another disastrous mistake and Bob's heroin addiction was stronger than his love for me. I began to feel uneasy and agitated again. I'd pace around the flat waiting for him to come home, then I'd quiz him, asking him where he'd been.

We started to drift apart; the mutual trust that had initially bonded us together had been broken. I must have appeared anxious and he didn't like it. He liked me the way I was in the early days, relaxed and easy going. He didn't like me being suspicious of him either. A judge was later to describe him as 'dangerous and evil', but at that time any feelings of misgiving I had towards him he quickly persuaded me were unfounded. We stayed together.

I was completely under Bob's influence, so when one day he offered me some of his physeptone linctus (a heroin substitute in a syrup), I took it. 'Try this and you'll feel mellow,' he said. It made me feel so good – I felt relaxed and able to cope with everything. I didn't feel afraid or anxious. It didn't matter then if he went away for a few hours. So I started taking physeptone linctus every day. But soon it wasn't enough, and I begged Bob to give me some of his heroin.

At first he was reluctant. I'd like to think it was because he didn't want to see me addicted like he was, but in truth I think it was because he didn't want to share his prescription with me. I've learnt that drug addicts are notoriously selfish. His own habit was growing and he was having to steal to buy enough for himself. But one day, when we were out together in London with the children, I asked him again to give me some heroin. Whether it was because he felt sorry for me, or whether it was because I'd worn him into the ground, he agreed.

So we found a quiet but dismal place, on the flat roof of a derelict office block. Bonita was in her pram asleep, and Chay amused himself while we sat on a stone step between some tall chimney stacks. Bob injected the heroin into my arm. It was over in seconds. I'd had my first fix. The next day he gave me some more. It was November 1975 and I'd become a heroin addict.

At first I didn't feel any benefit. But after a couple of days I started to notice how different I felt. I was on a cloud, floating from one thing to the next. I was untroubled, my mind was calm. I didn't feel worried and weighed down with anxiety. It was such a relief. I didn't feel afraid any more. I'd found what I was looking for and had a measure of peace at last.

Once it was clear to Bob that I wanted a daily fix of heroin, he had to work out a way of getting it for me. He couldn't afford to share his heroin with me because by then he needed more for himself than his daily prescription allowed. A few days later he took me to Reece House in East Croydon, a clinic for drug addicts.

In those days it was extremely easy to get drugs on prescription. He made some marks on my arms to make it look as though I'd been injecting myself for some time, and that was all they looked at. I wasn't even given a blood test. People who were dealers used to go there and obtain prescriptions – some of them weren't even addicts. Bob told me what to say, and it was as easy as that. They gave me a prescription for far more heroin than I needed at that time. Bob was pleased. His plan had worked: now he had enough to feed his habit as well as mine, for a time at least.

I was in a quandary. On the one hand it was such a relief not to feel afraid, but on the other, at the back of my mind

I was uneasy, though I wouldn't really admit it to myself. I thought I was coping, but of course I wasn't. My social worker's notes reveal the true story. 'My immediate concern is for her children,' one part of her report read. 'She is a very loving and caring mother, but her addiction has led her into financial difficulties.'

All through the winter of 1975/76 I remained at home with the children. The electricity was disconnected because I couldn't afford to pay the account. Chay was becoming disturbed and frequently wet his bed at night. I found him difficult to handle and he was reluctant to go to nursery school.

I proved the saying 'love is blind', because throughout this downward spiral into drug abuse, I remained in love with Bob. If ever I doubted him, he reassured me. He was a step ahead of me the whole time, anticipating what was going to happen next, controlling, manipulating. The doctor at the clinic gave me a prescription for four tablets of diamorphine heroin a day straight off. Every day I used to pick up my syringes, files of water and swabs from the chemist in Redhill. I would drop Chay off at nursery school and then go and get my fix.

I carried on like this for some time. I thought no one would even have guessed I was taking drugs. As my heroin addiction grew, I still thought that I was in control. All I really cared about was not being afraid, although I wasn't voicing that then. Soon, what I was being given on prescription wasn't enough. I had to find a way of obtaining more.

Bob's habit had continued to grow as well and he started robbing chemists' shops again – something I'd found out he used to do before I met him. So my life acquired another bad element. I started stealing too. I thought nothing of going out in the middle of the night and putting a brick through a jeweller's window, grabbing a tray of gold rings and running off into the dark before the police could catch me.

The next day I'd go to Hatton Garden on the train and sell the gold before going to Piccadilly with my prescription. There I'd mingle with other drug addicts and dealers, and buy or swap something to mix with the heroin to make a cocktail. Sometimes Bob and I would go together and we'd buy some speed or cocaine to make the heroin go further.

Just like the drink, it was a growing dependency. After a time I had taken so much speed and heroin that my teeth started to crumble. I could no longer bite anything hard. I bit on something one day and my front teeth went to powder. I'd become a physical wreck. By then I'd also lost a lot of weight and only weighed five stone. My sole motivation was getting my next fix.

I saw some dreadful things at this time. On one occasion, after a day of drug dealing, we were travelling home on the train from London with one of our best friends. As we sat together in the carriage, our friend injected himself with some Chinese heroin that we'd bought in Piccadilly that day. It was our turn next, but he took the first fix. I saw him swell up and choke before my very eyes. He died because somebody had 'cut' the heroin with yeast to double their profits. What he thought was pure heroin was in fact 50 per cent yeast.

You'd have thought seeing things like this would put me off. But they didn't. It's insane when I think about it now. I was losing my children step-by-step, but it didn't stop me. I was missing them growing up, but it didn't stop me. I loved them, but I was on a downward collision course. I was out of control, but I just couldn't stop. And still I *thought* that I was in control. I believed

I was still coping with the children, still caring for them properly. We went out and did a lot of things together, but this came to an abrupt halt when my life finally hit the crash barriers.

Bob and I regularly robbed chemists. We worked well as a team. I remember one night – one of many – we took a garden spade and went to the back of a chemist. Bob prized open the back door of the shop with the spade and we stole the DDA (dangerous drugs) cabinet. We knew how not to get caught, so we buried the cabinet in some ground nearby and went back for it at a later date, when we could be sure the police weren't suspecting us for the robbery. Then we took the drugs home and sorted them out. Some we'd use ourselves, other stuff we'd sell.

I'd changed from the child who cared about other people into someone who didn't care about anything. I'd wait in the public ladies' loos for someone old to lock themselves in the cubicle next to mine. I'd see their handbag on the floor and, quick as a flash, I'd grab it and run off – just to get a fix.

We'd managed to avoid being caught by the police so far, but I knew we'd be found out sooner or later. By this time I was too frightened to go and open the door if somebody rang the doorbell. I made people shout their name through the letter box before I let them in so that I could be sure who they were.

As 1976 drew on I became more and more frightened – no drugs could mask that feeling of continual, dragging fear. By September I was seriously thinking about committing suicide. I had plenty of drugs in the flat and knew I could take an overdose at any time to escape from the hell around me. I'd lost all control of the children. Then one evening the chip pan ignited and set fire to the kitchen. The neighbours telephoned the police and I was taken, unconscious, to Redhill General Hospital under Section 29 of the 1959 Mental Health Act.

They kept me in intensive care for one and a half days before I discharged myself against medical advice. Bob came to visit me and took me home. I thought he loved me, but in reality he needed my prescription for more heroin.

Meanwhile, the children had been placed in Robinsfield Children's Home in Caterham for a couple of days before being taken to my parents' house in Carshalton. Somehow, though, I summoned up the energy to fetch them home again. By this time Chay was even more disturbed and was wetting himself during the day as well as the night. The Educational Welfare Officer made an appointment for him to go to the Redhill Child Guidance Centre.

By October that year the situation had deteriorated still further and Bob attracted the attention of the Police Drug Unit based in Guildford. I noticed they had started to tail him and warned him, but it was too late. The police came and raided my flat. Bob and I were arrested, then bailed pending further charges. We'd always agreed that if Bob got caught I'd say the stuff was mine. I'd never been in trouble with the police before and I had two kids, so, we reasoned, they were bound to treat me leniently.

When the police searched the flat they found whole bags full of tablets. I had drugs in my washing machine. I had a bottle of cocaine at the back of my cooker. Other drugs were stuffed into my daughter's dolls. It took three officers three days to count all the pills. When they took me into the charge room and I looked at all the bags full of coloured tablets, I thought I was looking at someone else's work, so detached from the problem did I feel. I really didn't think anything would happen to me because this was my first offence. How wrong I was.

The court case was arranged for Monday 24 January 1977 at the new Kingston Crown Court. The court heard how 24-year-old Bob had peddled more than half his heroin prescription to fellow addicts, who would wait for him outside a chemist. Apparently he received 21 tablets of heroin a week and made a profit of about £30 a week from the ones he sold. The case was adjourned while Judge John Ellison ordered an investigation to find out how Bob was being prescribed a double heroin dose.

When the case came back to court in March, Judge Ellison said, 'This is an unusually complicated case. The couple have been dabbling with dangerous drugs, they've been supporting each other in evil. She married at 18 and now has two children. It is too dreadful to contemplate those children being brought up in an atmosphere of drugs. Boorer [my married name] has shown a determination to throw off drugs and I don't think she would be in this position today if [Bob] hadn't been around. I view [Bob] as a thoroughly dangerous man.'

I pleaded guilty to dishonestly obtaining a drugs prescription and to unlawful possession of 90 tablets of Ritalin, a controlled drug. Bob was jailed for three years and I was given a two-year suspended sentence with an order that I should receive medical treatment as an in-patient for at least one year.

I agreed to enter Cane Hill Hospital, in Coulsden, Surrey, for treatment regarding my drug problem. In early June, however, I discharged myself and ran away. The police were informed and I was taken back. But I ran away again the next day and hid in my flat. When I look back on this period of my life now, it's a blur of memories, a living nightmare. I went to find my children, but I was incapable of caring for them properly. I was also drinking heavily.

A neighbour reported that she'd seen Chay and Bonita taking bacon from the dustbin and eating it. She was prepared to substantiate her statements and as a result the Probation Officer was informed. The neighbour came up with some more stories and the social workers organized a 'case conference' for the second week in July. However, by the middle of June the children had already been taken into care again. It was decided that they should be looked after by my parents.

The social worker's report from that time is awful to read now:

> The flat was in an extremely dirty and disorderly state. The hall was swimming in water, as was the bedroom and the bathroom. The cause related to the bath tap having been left on and the bath containing dirty clothing. The water had dripped through to the floor below. The kitchen was dirty and the sink was full of dirty crockery and utensils, and the door to the fridge was hanging off. In the main bedroom the water was covering the floor and there was dirty clothing all around. The windows and curtains were tightly closed and under the bed there was thick dust. Found in the dust was a fireman's axe and two large knives. The most disturbing finds were in relation to two dirty syringes and a tourniquet found in the bedroom and the living room. A fire seemed to have been started in the lounge from old newspapers and rubbish.

I swore at and fought with the policemen who came to take my children away, and was charged with assault and of being under the influence of drink and drugs. I appeared in court again on 15 August 1977 and was placed on probation for two years, with the additional condition that I reside at Cane Hill Hospital for 12 months. So I was taken once again to the Cane Hill Drug Unit.

It was always the intention of those whose care I was in that I should be rehabilitated and encouraged to look after my children again. The social workers thought it would be a good idea if they found me another flat away from the scene of the drug taking. By November that year my few belongings had been moved to a flat in Sutton and arrangements had been put in place for me to see my children regularly.

But drink was my constant enemy. Every time I was allowed out of Cane Hill for a few hours I'd get drunk. On a couple of occasions I was involved with the police and appeared in court on drinking charges and fined.

Every time this happened I was returned to Cane Hill, and every time I ran away. I had clearly broken my two-year suspended sentence, so I was taken back to court and remanded in custody. It was 7 February 1978, and I was admitted to Holloway prison.

I was taken down the stairs at the back of the courtroom, put in a van and taken straight to Holloway. I'd already started having fits because, with no drugs available, I'd gone into withdrawal during the day. I had one fit in the courtroom, so I was taken straight to the hospital wing of the prison. They put me in a cell with just a mattress on the floor. They told me the next morning that I'd had 22 fits during the night. I don't remember any of it. It's a total blank.

sIX

Horror in Holloway

Holloway prison was a great shock to me. Nothing could have prepared me for it. I suppose I never really expected to be sent there. Bob had told me I'd be treated leniently by the judge, and I was still clutching at the plans we'd made. After all, I told myself, Bob had controlled my life for the past few years – I'd given up taking responsibility for my actions long ago. It had been easier to do what he said and go along with his schemes. I had trusted him and allowed myself to be completely under his influence.

The drugs and alcohol had obviously dulled my powers of reasoning. Far from providing me with the peace of mind and sense of well-being which had been promised at first, they had ruined my life. Now I'd lost everything and everyone I cared about. The starkness of my new situation hit me. I'd been living in unreality, but now the truth had caught up with me and I felt abandoned and very frightened. I was completely alone, having to take sole responsibility and pay a high price for my criminal activities.

Being sent to Holloway was like stepping into a living nightmare. Was it really me experiencing these things? How could this be? Where had things gone so wrong? Those first nights in prison were terrifying. My body cried out for more heroin, but there was none. I suffered alone and as the withdrawal process took its own painful time to pass, in its wake came the full realization of what had happened to my life.

I'd been heading for trouble for years. The road I'd been travelling along had led directly to this. I should have realized sooner. I'd already lost many of my friends – they had died because of the drugs they had been taking. I was still alive, but was as good as dead.

I'd made so many mistakes, hadn't even understood that people were trying to help me. I'd been put on probation for two years in August 1977. The first year was meant to be spent at Cane Hill, where the doctor responsible for me would either transfer me to another hospital if necessary or discharge me when I was considered well enough to leave. The second year I was supposed to be 'on probation' under the care and supervision of a Probation Officer in the community.

After the court hearing I'd been taken straight to Cane Hill, but I'd walked out immediately and gone to the pub for a drink. Maybe it was that drink that finally sent me on the road to Holloway. Certainly I'd been warned by the hospital staff and my social worker not to leave the hospital and on no account to enter a pub and buy a drink. They told me what the consequences would be.

They took me back to Cane Hill. I ran away again. I broke my promises, but they were true to their word. I'd been warned and now here I was, locked away in unfamiliar surroundings. I couldn't believe this had happened to me.

On top of the general shock, I was suffering withdrawal symptoms from the heroin, so I was kept in the hospital wing of the prison the whole time. The cells were quite modern, but as I lay on the mattress and looked at the windows I thought how intimidating they looked.

They were only a few inches wide and very tall. I could hardly see out of them and they served as a constant reminder that I was behind bars. I was locked in with no means of escape, and at that point I had no idea how long I would be held there.

For a first-timer like me it was simply a case of survival and learning how to cope. As my mind slowly cleared I discovered that the women who had been in Holloway for some time had developed some ingenious ways of communicating. Most of the inmates wore long maxi-cardigans, which they used to lower from window to window with notes in the pockets. Drugs were readily available for those who wanted them. Heroin injected into fresh oranges and brought in by relatives and friends provided those inside with a steady supply.

I met a girl in Holloway called Maria, and her experience was much the same as mine. She too had been very much in love with her boyfriend and had been manipulated as a result. Another girl, Lynne, was a very high class prostitute. She had devised a crafty way of earning a lot of money. She was very tall, very thin and very beautiful, and she just rolled men for their money. Every night she'd take her clients to a five-star hotel and while they were getting undressed she'd run off with their wallets. She had lived a life that was really dangerous.

I met another girl called Rocky and she was there because she'd tried to kill her stepmother. She and her close friend had stabbed this woman. It was a horrific attack and afterwards, believing her to be dead, they rolled her up in a carpet, put her in the boot of their car and drove her to a remote spot before rolling her body down a hill. But she wasn't dead – she survived and Rocky was arrested and charged with attempted murder. All I ever heard Rocky say about her was, 'It would have been worth it if she'd died.' I don't know what had happened to Rocky, but she was a sweet person.

As I came to my senses I couldn't stop thinking about Chay and Bonita. I was heartbroken at being separated from them and I didn't see them at all while I was in prison. I knew I hadn't been coping with life, but I loved them very much. I thought I'd provided for them. I'd tried my hardest to make sure they hadn't wanted for anything and had been well fed. But now I didn't know how they were and I missed them more than I can say. I no longer had a regular supply of heroin to mask the pain and the loss. Before long the awful reality of my desperate situation hit me really hard, and the toughest thing was being forcibly separated from my children.

I witnessed something in Holloway which showed me what can happen when someone misses their children so badly. One of the inmates was called Margaret and she had five children. She'd been charged with shoplifting – she'd been stealing to feed her kids. She needed help: I don't think she should have been sent to prison. She wasn't a danger to anybody! She was a very homely woman, rather frumpish, and she lived for her children. She couldn't stop talking about them.

She became very depressed and withdrawn in prison and one day she took a plastic knife from the canteen. She snapped the knife in two and in one move – it happened so quickly – she sawed straight through her windpipe and cut her jugular vein. We watched, horrified, as the blood gushed out of her like a fountain and splattered onto the floor.

She'd chosen to die rather than be separated from her children. It was awful and shocked us all. As I witnessed her suicide attempt and felt her despair, I knew that I deserved my punishment but she didn't. I'd done something wrong. All she'd done was steal some food to feed her children.

I can't begin to describe adequately the depths of emotion I witnessed in Holloway prison. Many of the women I met were lesbians. I heard them talking in the canteen or during the night, plotting their next crime so they could come back to prison to be with their lover. It was heartbreaking.

I missed my children immensely, but I came to realize that sanity lies in thinking ahead and not thinking back. Maybe it was the stark horror of Margaret's attempted suicide that jolted my mind into action, but I quickly became determined to get well. I had no drugs or alcohol in Holloway and the whole of my time there was spent in the hospital wing of the prison.

It was not a place that encouraged positive thought. There was nothing to do. We had no occupational therapy. We had one hour a day when we could watch television. Most of the time we were just locked in our cells. I smoked and learnt how to cut matchsticks to make six out of one. It was a wonderful education! I didn't receive any treatment and I wasn't seen by a psychiatrist. The only outside person I saw was my solicitor from time to time, because he was working really hard to secure my release. I wrote to my children, but I didn't get any replies.

The only positive aspect about being in Holloway was that it gave me some respite from a man who had been causing me considerable harm. He was a fellow patient I'd met while I was being treated at Cane Hill. I first met him about four months before I was sent to Holloway. Paul was an ex-drug addict. I was introduced to him at a group therapy session I attended at a hospital in Penge. The consultant responsible for my treatment in Cane Hill thought it would help in my recovery to attend this group, and so he arranged for me to be taken there each week.

At first I liked Paul. He was friendly. His marriage had failed and we seemed to have quite a lot in common. One lunchtime he invited me out for a drink. Although we knew this was strictly against the rules, we managed to slip out without being seen and he took me to his flat. It was there that he beat me up.

That was the first of many assaults. I can't understand now why I put up with his cruelty, but strangely enough it didn't put me off to begin with. Sometime later, after he'd subjected me to another severe beating, I saw my mother and she was so shocked at my injuries that she took me to the local hospital. Paul had stabbed me that time.

The doctor at the hospital informed the police and I was asked if I'd be prepared to bring charges against Paul. I wasn't. He'd beaten me very badly, but he was also very kind to me at other times. Apparently I reminded him of his mother – he said we looked alike. I didn't know the background story about Paul and his mother then, although I found out later. Besides, Paul held me in his influence because he'd told me he believed I should have my children back. At first I trusted him enough to think that he'd help me achieve this.

I was also influenced by the fact that Paul had been introduced to me by my consultant from Cane Hill. He'd suggested that Paul would be a good friend and counsellor for me, somebody I could talk to who would understand and empathize with my situation. So I thought it was worth putting up with the odd beating: if he was going to help me get my children back I couldn't afford to lose him.

But after he'd stabbed me, and might have killed me, any feelings I had for him quickly turned to terror. His behaviour had become obsessive. I started to feel like a hunted animal. I feared he'd come looking for me and I never wanted to see him again. It made me very frightened of spending any time in my own flat, even though the hospital staff were trying to rehabilitate me. The thought that Paul knew where to find me was enough to scare me into thinking that I never wanted to leave the safety of a locked ward or prison again. In that respect Holloway was a haven. But it wasn't long before he found me again.

Three weeks after being admitted to prison, my solicitor arranged for me to be transferred back to Cane Hill Hospital. I was taken under police escort and this time I was placed in a locked ward.

sEVEN

No way out

I was shut in Browning Ward at Cane Hill, a locked ward for convicted prisoners. There I was to undergo a few months' rehabilitation in the hope that I would then be able to resume a normal life with my children. I suppose they were doing their best, but little did I realize then that it would be four and a half years before I left hospital. During this time I lost what little dignity I had left.

My solicitor had fought to get my sentence changed because he didn't consider it was right for me to be in prison. He felt I needed psychiatric care and there wasn't any such help available in Holloway then. I wish now he'd left me in prison, because going back to Cane Hill was one of the worst things that happened to me.

At the time I was fairly positive because I thought I'd soon see my children again. I did. The day after I arrived from Holloway my mother walked in with Chay and Bonita, holding their hands. I was so pleased to see them. But as I got up to go over to them she looked at me and said, 'I've just come to tell you that today I've legally fostered them and you're never going to see them again.'

I could see that Chay wanted to run to me but he was really scared. We stood looking at each other for a few seconds. I was rooted to the spot. Then my mother spat at me before turning round and walking out, still holding onto the children's hands.

That prompted my first suicide attempt. I found a razor blade and cut my wrists open. I slit them as deeply as I could – I desperately wanted to die. In that moment, I felt the utter loneliness of despair. Far from taking a step towards recovering my children, every day seemed to pull them further away from me. I felt as though I was being torn into little pieces, and nobody cared.

I wasn't able to help myself. The people I trusted had let me down. There was nobody I could turn to. Nobody was on my side. Now even my own mother thought I was despicable and treated me with contempt. I was labelled as a drug addict, alcoholic and criminal in the hospital. I knew I couldn't exist without the drink. I was locked in a cage with no means of escape. All I wanted was to hold my children, to beg them to give me another chance.

I wanted to prove I could be a good mother again. I'd been a good mother for the first few years. In 1975, before I'd become a drug addict, one of my social workers had described me as 'a very loving and caring mother'. But now, just three years later, it felt as though everything I treasured had been snatched from me and it had all happened so quickly. Now I was unloved, untrusted, with everything to prove to people who didn't believe in me. I could see no way of escape, and my future looked bleak.

My time in Browning Ward was a deeply unsettling experience. I was locked up with some extremely violent patients. Sometimes they were violent towards me and sometimes they were loving. It was a schizophrenic existence and fear was my constant companion. How could I possibly recover my own balance in such an atmosphere?

I was encouraged to go out for a weekend every now and then to stay with my mother and the rest of the family. The idea was that I should go and see my children and rebuild my relationship with them in an unthreatening environment. But the moment I left the hospital I'd get drunk and when I arrived at my mother's house she wouldn't let me talk to the children. She wouldn't even let me near them. She certainly wouldn't let me eat with them.

I soon realized that she'd told the family many terrible things about me, stories that I knew weren't true. So now even my own brothers and sisters turned against me and nobody would talk to me, let alone listen to me. Visits like this did nothing to help my confidence and the emotional pressure just made me crumble inside. After a weekend like this I'd return to the hospital and never want to go out again. It was easier to be locked up. I didn't want to leave the prison that had become the safest place I knew.

I was also afraid to go back to my own flat in case Paul found me. I lived in terror of ever seeing him again. Each attack on me had been worse than the one before. I reasoned that it was only a matter of time before he killed me altogether.

Despite this, those looking after me at Cane Hill were still keen to encourage me to spend a few hours each week away from the hospital. They found me a small flat at Mill Green where I was encouraged to spend my weekends. They were trying to ease me out, to build up my confidence and help me stand on my own two feet again, so that eventually I could be reunited with my children and look after them myself. I knew they were trying to help me, but there seemed to be so many obstacles in the way.

I persevered in spite of the difficulties and my acute sense of fear. One weekend I was alone in the flat. At about half past two in the morning I was woken by the sound of somebody kicking the front door. I saw a man's hand come through a hole in the door. The safety chain was on, but he ripped it off. It was Paul.

To this day I don't know how he found out my where-abouts. I was only there for the weekend, trying to see my children and show that I could manage to live by myself.

Paul raped me, then he stabbed me 27 times through the chest and breast with a long stiletto knife before leaving me for dead. During the last two of those stabbings I just didn't move. I survived by pretending I was dead.

I remember very little of what happened after that. A neighbour raised the alarm, and when the police arrived they found Paul sitting on the floor in the hallway covered in blood. I was rushed to hospital, drifting in and out of consciousness. Eighteen of my wounds had to be stitched.

After this traumatic experience I was moved to Netherne Hospital, where I came under the care of Dr Raymond, a consultant psychiatrist. I was still drinking heavily and had been warned that if I continued with this lifestyle I'd be dead before long. I didn't care. I wanted to die. I had nothing left to live for.

Netherne was a large hospital for the mentally ill, close to Cane Hill. I was put into Hartswood Villa, where we were encouraged to work. We were offered menial jobs, either packing plastic spoons into bags or sewing sanitary towels, for which we were paid about £4.00 a week.

During the week we worked from nine in the morning until four in the afternoon, with an hour off for lunch. Every day we were given tablets. I suppose they were intended to keep us sedated, but the side effects were unpleasant and my weight almost doubled to 12 stone. The combination of being depressed and knowing I looked ugly and fat did nothing for my self-esteem.

I developed what I called the 'Netherne Shuffle'. I can always tell someone who has been in a hospital like Netherne or who has been on these tablets because they walk differently!

I had a dear friend in Netherne called Barry – he was just such a gentle chap. There was no romantic attachment, he was just a good, dependable, reliable friend who made no emotional demands on me. He suffered from schizophrenia and his mother owned the shop at the bottom of the drive.

Barry threw himself off a bridge and fell under the London-to-Brighton train. The tablets we were all given had affected him badly, perhaps, and he'd been depressed because he hadn't got enough money to buy 10 fags. I walked down the drive to the bridge the next morning and as I looked at the railway line I saw that part of his tartan jacket was still hanging there.

It wasn't uncommon for that sort of thing to happen, or for people to take an overdose, just because they didn't have enough money to buy their fags. Cigarettes were a valuable commodity in Netherne. Women had sex with men just to get a fag. All everyone thought of was getting hold of the next fag. We even emptied the rubbish out of the dustbins to find the dog-ends.

Barry just didn't have enough money to buy cigarettes that day. Looking back, I wouldn't describe the mundane work we did as occupational therapy. The patients didn't get much out of it – rather it lined the pockets of the local firms. Being 'mental' doesn't mean things cost you less money.

I later read a newspaper report about his death:

A young man's body may have been hit by two trains before it was discovered on the line at Netherne,

Hooley. Barry John Webster's body was strewn over a distance of 200 yards before a train driver saw there had been an accident and raised the alarm. Dr Peter Pullar, pathologist from Guy's Hospital, said Mr Webster, aged 26, died from multiple injuries after the fall on September 10, 1978. There was no trace of alcohol in the blood. Train driver, Mr Ray Emm, said he saw a body lying on the line near the Ford Bridge. 'The body was lying on the line when I came along,' he said. Reigate Coroner's Court heard that Mr Webster had been receiving treatment at Netherne Hospital since November 1976. A report from a Netherne doctor, not named by the court, said Mr Webster had given him no cause for concern. He did a certain amount of work very well. There was no sign of distress or anything to cause concern. Before the jury returned an open verdict on the cause of Mr Webster's death, the coroner, Lieutenant Colonel George McEwan, said the man suffered from schizophrenia. (*Surrey Mirror*, 27 October 1978)

What a cold report, I thought. They didn't understand in the slightest what it was like in Netherne. And I'd lost a friend.

I continued to go to work every day, without Barry. One of the doctors discovered I could use a typewriter, so he gave me a thesis to type. He told me I did it well. The word went round, and before long another doctor asked me to type a thesis for him. In return they gave me boxes of chocolates or money, which I saved until I had enough to buy Chay and Bonita some Christmas presents.

I improved sufficiently for them to allow me home for a weekend and it was arranged that I would visit Chay and

Bonita at my mother's house. The day arrived. I was taken there in a taxi, along with all the parcels I'd been getting ready for weeks. I'd spent many hours wrapping them carefully, making them look as attractive and surprising as I could.

I was really looking forward to seeing the children again, and I felt sure they would be pleased to see me. But when my mother opened the door she screamed at me and scratched her face, then yelled that I'd hurt her. Slamming the door in my face, she ran through the hallway, grabbed my two children and held them up to a window.

She seemed to be laughing at me. I stood outside looking at my children's faces, the tears stinging in my eyes. She wouldn't let me in. I walked all the way back to Netherne from Carshalton. I left the presents lying in the front garden and later learnt that they'd been burnt.

For a while I was numb, but it wasn't long before I reacted and went berserk. I screamed and cried. I'd wanted to see Chay and Bonita so badly – I'd wanted to hold them and hug them, to tell them I loved them and wanted us to live together again. Instead I ended up with a needle in my backside.

When I woke up from the sedation I found I was in John Ward, a locked ward in Netherne, and that's where I stayed for a few weeks. I think at this stage I almost completely lost my will to live. I started treating myself badly.

I learnt things in Netherne in the same way that you learn things in prison: by watching other people. When I first went into Netherne I was horrified at some of the things I witnessed. It had happened to a lesser extent in Cane Hill, but the people were older there and that seemed to make a difference. Sex had been high on the agenda at Cane Hill, but in Netherne people hurt themselves. Every day, maybe three or four times a day, someone would put their fist through a window and slam their wrist down on the jagged glass. People would run to pick up the pieces of glass and hide them. Then, when they were ready, they'd use the jagged fragments of glass to cut themselves in the privacy of their own cubicle.

I don't know why I started doing it. Perhaps I thought people would feel sorry for me; perhaps I thought my mum would care more if I hurt myself. I don't know, but in the end it became an obsession with me. The only time I felt clean was after I'd cut myself. I think this is where I ended up becoming a very, very sick person. I hated myself and cut myself regularly. I don't mean just a little bit – I laid myself open to the bone. I'd just saw away at my flesh with a piece of glass. The only time I ever felt that I'd punished myself properly for what I'd done to my children was when I bled.

I can't adequately describe the despair of being in hospital, separated from Chay and Bonita, loving them but not being able to prove it. It seemed to me then that each time I started to recover and get close to my kids again, something went wrong and I was thrown back into a deep, dark hole.

It's strange now to think that even when my mind was dulled by drink and drugs I still believed that the only way I could pay for the wrong I'd done was to shed my own blood. I really hated myself and did all I could to destroy my body. But it wasn't just myself that I hated.

I started to have fantasies about my mother and often dreamt that I was like Ruth Ellis. In my dreams I'd walk up to my mum's front door and knock. When she opened it I'd shoot her straight between the eyes. Then I'd sit down and tell myself that now the whole world was safe.

I also wondered what would have happened if Chay and Bonita had been taken into a children's home to be cared for. Would it have made any difference? But however hard I thought, I couldn't find a solution. After all, I was the one who'd been taking drugs and drinking; I was obviously the guilty party. I felt trapped and doomed to spend the rest of my life in a mental hospital.

Today, with the benefit of hindsight, I don't hate my mother. I can see now that she's had just as sad a life as me. She was a victim of her circumstances; it was a case of history repeating itself. What would it take to break the cord of tragedy that had threaded itself down through the generations of our family? Who could help us? As hard as I thought, I couldn't understand why things had gone so badly wrong.

I had nobody who would listen to me. The only person who came to visit me occasionally was my mother herself. Sometimes, despite what she'd said, she did bring Chay and Bonita with her. But I felt it was always awkward and after she'd gone I felt sad and empty and wished she'd stayed away. Seeing Chay and Bonita just emphasized the hopelessness of my situation. It was so tantalizing, but after a short time they were always taken away again. The reality of my loss was too hard to bear.

So I just existed from day to day. I had no confidence in myself and agoraphobia was my constant unwelcome companion. The only way I could keep sane was to prevent myself from thinking too deeply. I was prescribed strong tranquillizers. Drugs were my only friend.

eIGHT

So close to hope

After his vicious attack on me, Paul Herrick was charged with attempted murder and sentenced to five years in prison. I was safe at last, at least for a time. But the memory of that night haunted me for months afterwards. The wounds healed, but the scars remained – scars that were etched deep into my memory. The man my doctor had thought could help and encourage me, the man he'd persuaded me to be on friendly terms with, was the man who eventually raped and stabbed me and left me for dead. After that attack, it was six months before I felt confident enough to leave Netherne for a weekend and stay in my flat by myself.

I suppose I must have been in shock for a long time. As I sat and relived the nightmare of that attack and looked at the scars on my body, I was reminded that someone I'd thought was a friend had almost killed me. At the time I didn't know why he'd attacked me. He'd called me Josephine during the assault. I later discovered his mother's name had been Josephine and she'd been murdered when he was a boy – stabbed to death in her kitchen with a carving knife. Apparently, the theory was that Paul had killed her, although it had never been proved.

The nursing staff at Netherne encouraged me to begin the rehabilitation process all over again, but I was really frightened and had no confidence in my ability to cope. What would happen the next time I was alone in the outside world? I felt a complete wreck and had no sense of self-esteem. And I concluded that the assault didn't look good on my record – all it had done was to provide more ammunition for my mother.

My relationship with Paul had driven a further wedge between my mother and me. I felt she was more convinced than ever that I was totally irresponsible and quite incapable of ever looking after my children again. In her eyes I was clearly unable to choose 'suitable' friends. This only served to make my depression worse. Persuading her to trust me again, enough to agree to me having my children back, seemed an impossibility. I drank to dull my pain and despair. So far, I told myself, everybody I'd trusted to help me had let me down.

I came to the negative conclusion that my mother must think I was always going to invite men like that to my flat. In her opinion, therefore, the children would continually be in danger when they visited me. Maybe she thought I mixed with disreputable people because all I cared about was having sex. I felt I was in an impossible situation; it was a constant nightmare with no hope of escape or change. I didn't know what to do. I was in a living hell. Nobody would believe me.

I heard that my mother had even written letters to Bob to tell him that I was seeing somebody else. Before this I had been taken to see Bob in prison. My mother came to see me one day and said, 'If you write and tell Bob that you're seeing someone else, I'll let you see the children.' Naively, I wrote the letter. I never got to see the children, though, and now I'd lost Bob as well. I never saw him again. I realized that yet again I'd allowed myself to be manipulated and misunderstood; even my own mother was against me.

In my mind she became my biggest enemy. I felt more threatened by her than by the men who'd abused me. At least they'd been caught and their crimes against me had been recognized. But it seemed that I was the only person who realized that my mother wasn't actually working *for* me. Yes, she was looking after my children, but only I knew how furious she was with me for what I'd done all those years ago in bringing the priest to the house and breaking the influence my father had over the family. I'd shattered her beliefs and existence then, and now I was spoiling her life all over again.

Today, from where I stand now, I understand that really she's a product of her own pain. But then, it seemed as though all her bitterness was being directed at me and I was paying the cost of her own difficulties.

Because of her scheming, I never saw Bob again – and after Paul's attack I felt I never wanted to leave the hospital anyway. If they could have brought Chay and Bonita to live with me I would have liked that, but I wanted to stay at Netherne because my fellow inmates had become my family. I felt safer with the lunatics than I did with the sane people. I was gripped by agoraphobia, which was masked to an extent by the drugs and drink, but the moment I was sober the fears would all come flooding back. So gradually I started to feel safe in Netherne. Situated as it was at the end of a mile-long drive, I felt cushioned from the outside world. I suppose I'd become institutionalized.

Meanwhile, the hospital doctors were gently trying to ease me out once again, to build up my confidence and help me to stand on my own two feet. They told me they still wanted me to be reunited with my children and able to look after them, and slowly I started to believe them. As the months passed, I began to improve. Progress was agonizingly slow, however, because I so disliked spending weekends in my flat, full of memories of the attack. I felt nervous every time I went there, especially when I was on my own.

I discussed this with my social worker, and I'd improved so much by October 1978 that a case conference was held at which they decided that I could be discharged. They agreed that it would be sensible to find me somewhere else to live, so the Sutton Housing Department offered me alternative accommodation in the Carshalton area. They provided me with a semi-detached house with three bedrooms, a bathroom and a large garden. It was in a quiet residential neighbourhood and I felt really enthusiastic about its potential, although the house needed a considerable amount of redecoration and modernization.

It was agreed that I should be allowed to have the two children home for trial periods, provided there was adequate supervision. They obviously considered that I'd made good progress! And I suppose I had. Having been almost killed earlier in the year, I'd fought my way back to health and strength. The only reason I'd bothered to do so was in the hope that I could be reunited with Chay and Bonita. Things were starting to look up. At last I felt I had a chance, and I focused all my energies on getting better.

I spent considerable amounts of time at the house making improvements, creating a homely atmosphere that I thought Chay and Bonita would like. I replaced the carpets, decorated the rooms and scrounged some pieces of furniture. My social worker was pleased with my progress and considered it was time the children started to come and stay with me for weekends.

I was no longer taking drugs and tried hard to co-operate with my social worker. I was often impatient with him, though! I sometimes felt things were happening too slowly. However, we spent the Christmas of 1978 together and at the end of January I asked if the children could come and live with me permanently. Everything seemed to be going well, so it was agreed that they could return for the half-term holiday in February and then again for the entire Easter holiday.

I don't know what went wrong. I had one drink to help me over the anxiety I was feeling on a particular day. I think it was due to the agoraphobia. The only way I could stay calm was by having a drink. I'd been unable to control the children that day. They'd been naughty and daubed paint around the house and made it look very untidy, which upset me dreadfully. One drink led to another, and before long I was denied my children again. They were taken to Butlins for a holiday with my parents and I was taken back into hospital for a month.

Back at Netherne, I thought about how close I'd come to making a success of looking after Chay and Bonita again. I realized after talking to my social worker that I probably had a fetish about not allowing the house to get dirty or untidy in case the children were taken away again. I told myself that I wouldn't lose control in that way again; by the time they returned from their holiday I'd be able to cope and we could be together again. I started to look forward to their return.

It was a huge blow to be told I couldn't have them back as I'd hoped. They were to return to live with my parents during the week while I attended the Day Hospital in the Chiltern Wing of Sutton Hospital. I'd come so close to getting it right. Was I now about to lose it all again?

I don't remember much about the next few months. I wasn't allowed to see the children on my own and access was only permitted through visits to my parents' house. I made no secret of the fact that I wanted to die. Once again, drugs and drink became my solace.

I didn't really like Dr Raymond, the consultant psychiatrist from Netherne, until the day in September 1979 when I made another serious attempt to take my life. Alone in the house, I took 80 paracetamol tablets washed down by three pints of milk. Then I cut my wrists open with a razor until I had no power left in my hands. This time – surely – I would die.

I'm not sure what happened then. I soon slipped into unconsciousness, but I was found the next day and taken to hospital. By that time so many hours had elapsed that the hospital warned my mother that my liver and kidneys were seriously damaged. It was quite possible that I might die.

I was taken to the operating theatre where my wrists were stitched back together again. I had my arms in plaster for three and a half months after that. I woke up in intensive care with complete kidney and liver failure. As I opened my eyes and slowly focused on my surroundings, the first person I saw was Dr Raymond. I'd always thought he was so hard, but he said to me then, 'Oh Angie, why?' He was holding my hand and I could see he'd been crying.

By that simple act he helped me more than he knew, because it showed me he cared. Apparently he'd been sitting there for a very long time before I woke up. Up to that point I didn't think anyone cared about me. In fact, I thought they'd be better off without me. That must have been due to a hardness within me. I hadn't seen this side of Dr Raymond before. To me he'd just been the enemy. But now something was different in the way he related to me.

This change had taken place because, when the doctors thought I was going to die, they'd called my mother to the hospital. Dr Raymond was there when she arrived. He'd watched her walk in and take a look at me (I was bright yellow with jaundice) before quickly walking out again. I think it would have suited her if I'd died.

Dr Raymond sat and talked with me for a long time and I felt that at last he understood my situation. Now I had a friend who would help me and whom I could trust. That experience was a real turning point for me. It was the first time, I thought, that anyone had believed me. He talked to me and we went back over my case history. Slowly I started to feel a little bit better as I began to believe I had something to hang on to.

Dr Raymond said to me that I needed to go back to Netherne for at least six months because I was so traumatized, I wouldn't survive outside. He told me, 'If you leave here now, you'll go and get drunk, because underneath nothing has changed to alter all those fears. We need to sort through all that's happened with your past.'

So the arrangements were made. I didn't resist because I believed that Dr Raymond was on my side now. He'd understood my frustration, my struggle. He'd witnessed me almost winning my children back. He'd registered my mother's outrage at my behaviour and her impatience at the effect I was having on her life.

Sutton Council agreed to take back the house in Courtney Crescent, Carshalton, and in exchange provided me with a one-bedroomed flat in Sutton. It was explained to me that my children would not be returning to me in the foreseeable future. That was a bitter pill to swallow.

nINE

Roller
coaster ride

For the next six months I was denied access to Chay and Bonita. They went to live once again with my parents in Carshalton. I felt as though the relationship with my mother had reached an all-time low. Instinctively I knew she didn't trust me and probably never wanted to see me again. I suppose I was an inconvenience to her. I certainly believed she was disappointed I hadn't died; if I had she would have had one less problem to deal with.

From my weak, pathetic perspective she was the impenetrable barrier preventing me from ever getting my children back. If it hadn't been for the fact that Dr Raymond understood my feelings of anxiety and despair towards my mother, I would have made another suicide attempt. All my life it had been her word against mine, and up to this point she had always been the winner.

Each time I had come tantalizingly close to getting better, the loss of being repeatedly separated from the two people I loved had overwhelmed me. Could I cope with yet another disappointment? For days I wondered if it was worth the effort of trying to pick myself up and start all over again. Each time it was harder. The fear of another failure, coupled with my own self-doubt as to whether I really had it in me to succeed and be strong enough to stop drinking, made the situation seem hopeless.

Yet something had changed. This time I had a thread of hope. After all those years of being disbelieved, I felt that I now had somebody who had listened properly to my story. Dr Raymond was the only person I trusted. Nothing was going to be easy, though. Dr Raymond suggested I get involved with some group therapy. But I couldn't be bothered talking to a group; it seemed pointless. I wasn't prepared to play games. To me group therapy sessions were just excuses for sitting around and telling jokes. What use was that to me? Besides, after my experience with Paul, I was too wary to trust anybody I didn't know.

Also, years of punishment had taken their toll on my psyche. I'd come to believe that I was the one who was guilty and wrong. I hated myself because of the way I'd let my children down. I loved them, but I'd hurt them so much. I couldn't think of one reason why I should like myself, so I'd chosen to hate myself instead. And in making that choice I'd almost killed myself by cutting my legs, my arms and my body; I'd sliced it to pieces.

I thought about these things as I recovered from my suicide attempt, sitting helplessly with my arms in plaster. The long battle fought itself slowly out in my mind. I had to decide if the glimmer of hope I thought I'd seen was genuine. If it was, I then had to learn to change my pattern of thinking completely. I had six months to do it in, before my case was reviewed again.

Dr Raymond arranged for me to spend weekends in a house close to where my children were living, in Carshalton Beeches, rather than spending all the time at my little flat. I wasn't sure how my family would react if they heard I was living nearby. I feared they wouldn't be pleased and my fears were soon justified.

I was alone when it happened. My brothers came and trashed my house. They urinated on the beds; they broke all the toys I'd collected; they wrecked the whole house. I didn't tell anybody about what they'd done because of Chay and Bonita. I didn't want anything to happen to them. Added to that, they were still my brothers: I'd brought them up and I didn't want to get them into trouble. After all, I decided, nobody would have believed me – it was my word against theirs.

For the rest of that weekend I got drunk. And this started to become the pattern again: every time I was let out of hospital I drank. I wasn't thinking very clearly; I felt so afraid and alone. I'd chosen once again to isolate myself and manage the whole problem on my own. I didn't believe I had anything to gain by confiding in anyone. I was still taking a lot of prescribed drugs, but I was drinking as well now. I was drinking to summon up the courage to go back to that house, which, of course, was totally counterproductive to what the staff at Netherne were trying to do for me.

I should have realized my behaviour would soon be noticed. I got so drunk one weekend that I fell asleep too close to the electric fire. I was wearing lycra leggings. They caught fire and I nearly lost my leg, it was so badly burned. It wasn't long before I lost that house and it too was handed back to the council.

Once again, another opportunity had been quickly lost and I was back full time in Netherne Hospital. Dr Raymond's plan had been for my mother, in time, to bring the children over to the house to stay with me, initially for a few hours, so that we could get to know each other again. But left unsupervised, this scheme simply hadn't worked.

I was permanently terrified, but I found that hard to admit. I also found it difficult to tell the staff at Netherne what my brothers had done. How could they be expected to understand and help if I only gave them part of the story? I saw Dr Raymond very little after this, as I felt I'd let him down. So once again, I didn't have anybody to turn to whom I trusted. I became even more introverted. I didn't talk very much to anybody. I lived in fear of going home and started drinking as soon as I left the hospital grounds. And then I started drinking in the hospital.

Everything went crazy in my head. I wasn't behaving like the kind of person who really should be given a chance to have some time with her children. I didn't deserve it, I thought in despair. I didn't deserve to have them with me because I wasn't capable at that point of looking after them. By this time Chay was 11, and Bonita 9 years old. I lost all hope and just kept wishing they'd left me in Holloway. It seemed as though I was doomed to go round and round in these circles, looping from hope to despair and back again, each time just missing the goal.

Then something happened that did make a big difference to my life. Although I was very hurt at the time, and the immediate aftermath was appalling, I've since wondered if it wasn't something God allowed to happen. I can now see that I would never have got out of Netherne otherwise. I kept making mistakes and getting hauled back. A couple of times I was even taken to Sutton Hospital because I was in such a state. By now I had again been denied all access to my children because of my behaviour. I was arrested on more than one occasion for being drunk and disorderly in the street.

One night I was taken back to Netherne having been found wandering around Sutton. As I climbed blearily into bed I felt a piece of paper under my pillow. Curious, I unfolded it. Slowly I realized that it was a love letter to me from one of the charge nurses. He'd just started working at the hospital. At this time I was still recovering from the serious burn on my leg. It was taking a long time to heal and this man had been put in charge of taking care of me and changing the dressing regularly.

I read the letter, and that was it. I didn't need drink any more – I was in love. You see, that's what I was like then. I was all right as long as I had a crutch. The letter invited me to meet him at the bottom of the stairs the next evening. 'I am going to take you out of here my princess,' the letter read.

So, the next night, at one o'clock in the morning, I crept out of bed and along the corridors to the back door. He had a car and we drove up to London, where he treated me to a meal. Then he took me back to the hospital again and I crept into my bed in the early hours of the morning.

This became a regular pattern. I stopped drinking and started to take care of myself again. And everybody noticed. 'She's in love, you know!' they all said. I did feel different, I felt so different. I started to lose weight. I also started to spit pills out because I didn't want them. I started to regain some pride in my appearance.

We had to keep our liaison a secret or he would have been sacked. He used to drive me to Covent Garden and take me out for a meal, and then sneak me into the hospital through the back way. It was really exciting! Here I was, going out with a tall hunk of a man (he was six foot six; I'm only five foot one!) who cared only about me. He was playing a dangerous game and putting his job on the line for me. I believed he loved me. It quickly developed into a sexual relationship and he became everything I felt I needed. Just like the drink, he could calm me. I liked him so much, I didn't mind if he only wanted me for sex, so long as I thought he loved me too.

After a few weeks I frightened the life out of him. He came to pick me up one evening and I'd packed my bags. I put them in the car and said, 'Please take me to my flat.' That night I left Netherne for good – I just walked out. He couldn't really stop me because he wasn't meant to be seeing me in the first place. He couldn't risk making a scene because other people would have heard and the night staff were nearby in the office.

He stayed with me that night in my flat in Sutton. I was ecstatic. I thought he was the man of my dreams. He didn't beat me. He didn't give me drugs. I wasn't drinking. He appeared to care for me and love me too.

The next morning he went off to work, while I stayed at home and prepared an evening meal for him. I made the flat and myself look as romantic as I could! But when he came back that evening I was in for a nasty surprise.

I knew the moment he walked through the door that something was wrong. He seemed agitated and went straight to the point. He told me I'd misunderstood his intentions and announced that he was engaged to be married. Of course I hadn't known this. I was devastated. He'd given me a reason to live again and now he was about to walk out of my life, leaving me nowhere, with no support.

Alone again, I started to drink. Nobody came looking for me. Alcoholics have a saying, 'Poor me, poor me, pour me another drink.' There's a different mind-set with an alcoholic. We make friends with people and then cause them to hurt us. We make them angry with us just so that we can say, 'There, even they've let me down,' and that gives us the excuse we're looking for to go and pour another drink.

Therefore, because nobody from Netherne came to look for me, and I'd thought they were my family, for months I used that as a reason to drink. I suppose they weren't really worried about me because I hadn't been held there under section – I was there voluntarily. I'd been off-section for about two years by then. I'd stayed there because I just couldn't imagine being anywhere else, and yet I didn't want to be there at all. It sounds so pathetic, but it was the safest place I knew on the face of the earth. Well, I wasn't there now. I'd walked out. And there was no one else to care for me.

The flat I was in then was a small studio flat. It was tucked away on a floor of its own with its own small landing, so it was quite a spooky place. It was in a big block of flats in Sutton called Killick House. I had two heavy swing doors to go through and it was scary because I never knew who would be hanging about in the corridors and landings, especially at night. The entrance area was badly lit and the streetlights cast eerie shadows which often played tricks on my fertile imagination, further confused by drink.

Once I'd summoned the courage to stagger upstairs, it was with relief that I shut my front door behind me. I'd fall into a fitful sleep, only to be woken by nightmares. The neighbours would often report me to the police because they could hear me screaming in the middle of the night. I had no peace. Even in sleep I was tormented by memories and fears.

I was so often drunk. I had a little bit of social security money which I used to buy drink and when I didn't have any drink I stayed in bed. It was during this period that my drinking habit really took off.

Unbeknown to me, during this time my father had died suddenly. I wasn't told and the funeral went ahead without me being there. It was some time before I heard about his death, even though my mother and brothers knew where I was. Still nobody came to see me and still I was denied access to my children.

There was one good thing about living in Killick House, though: I was very close to my sister Pam. By now she was married with two children, Daniel and Jamie. I used to go to her home and she'd give me news about Chay and Bonita. But she was too frightened to tell my mother we were seeing each other, and couldn't really help me in any way. I'd caused my mother so much trouble that by this time I believed she really hated me. I'd become such a nuisance and embarrassment to her, and I was told that just the mention of my name made her angry. What would she do if she knew Pam was in contact with me?

Pam was having a difficult time herself. She'd just given birth to twins who had died, and she came home from hospital to find her husband had been accused of having an affair. Pam had a nervous breakdown when she heard this and was taken first to the Chiltern Wing, the psychiatric ward at Sutton Hospital where I'd spent many a month, and then to Netherne Hospital. Meanwhile, her two children, Daniel and Jamie, were taken to live with my mother.

So now my mother had control of Chay and Bonita *and* Daniel and Jamie. I may have been drinking heavily, but all of a sudden I realized I had to pull myself together to help Pam and stop this situation. I went to see her in hospital and brought her home to my flat. I knew where Tom would be: in the betting shop! I went and found him too and brought him to the flat.

I said to them, 'Just stay here until you've sorted it out. Go and get your kids, you bloody fools – can't you see, can't you see what's happening? Pam, you're going to end up in Netherne like me. You can't do this. I've lost my

kids, but you don't have to lose yours.' And they listened!
I let them stay in my flat and because I had nowhere else
to go I slept rough that night.

It worked. Pam and Tom sorted out their differences.
They went and fetched Jamie and Daniel and took them
home.

The thought of Pam going through what I'd been
through sent shockwaves of panic through me. It seemed
to me that history was about to repeat itself all over again.
I couldn't sit back and watch that happen. I may have
been drinking, but I did know by then that my circumstances weren't all my own fault. It wasn't until I became
a Christian, however, that I started to understand this
more fully and could look at my mother with pity. What
had happened to our family was no coincidence. In part it
was due to things that had happened long ago, habits and
wrong patterns of behaviour that had been passed down
the family lines to our own generation.

So Pam and Tom got their children back. I had
managed to sober up for a while when Pam needed me. It
showed at least that when I was needed or loved I could
put the bottle down. After that I had periods of really
trying to get myself together. I was told later on that's
what saved my life. But alone again, I couldn't keep it up
for long. What was the point? The curtains of despair
drew themselves around me and I was shrouded in a tent
of darkness and despair. Then the drinking just got worse
and worse and worse.

tEN

Rock bottom

One of the few things I could be certain of in my uncertain world was that by now the relationship with my mother had reached an all-time low. I sensed that she didn't want to see me at all. It must have been difficult for her, especially now that my father had died. She moved to a smaller house in Carshalton which, although it was no further away from me geographically, psychologically might as well have been on another planet. I could no longer imagine Chay and Bonita in surroundings familiar to me. I didn't know what their bedrooms looked like. I couldn't picture them in the kitchen or the garden. I certainly couldn't visit them.

For the next two years, 1982 to 1984, I existed in an alcoholic haze. As before I was often in trouble with the police for being drunk and disorderly on the streets. I was badly beaten up and admitted to St Helier Hospital on more than one occasion. It must have appeared that I was doing little to help myself.

I had a new social worker during this period. I met her when I was a day patient at Sutton Hospital. I used to go there and make candles and weave baskets – I don't quite know why! She seemed to take a genuine interest in my case and came to see me regularly. I thought she was stunningly beautiful and we became good friends. She was very young and, I suppose, inexperienced, but she was no fool.

She repeatedly took presents from me to my children, and my mother ripped them up in front of her, apparently saying that Chay and Bonita wanted nothing to do with me. Once my mother gave her a bag of ashes to bring back to me with the message, 'Tell her that's the remains of the other presents and if she wants to send any more say we could do with a fire.' I thought that was a very bold move on my mother's part. By behaving like that she was starting to reveal her true self to the authorities.

During these two years I did have good times when my drinking habit was under control. This usually coincided with meeting some man who'd offer to take me out. Inevitably sex was involved – it was the only form of payment I could afford. However, it seemed a valuable currency and one I became used to dealing in. As before, the moment anybody expressed any interest in me, the drinking would stop straight away. It was my usual habit, my usual way. But it generally wasn't long before I fell flat on my face again and the collapse would always occur after some incident connected with my mother.

I had a job working for the Sue Ryder Foundation and after a while I was made the manager of a charity shop in Sutton. From where I was coming from this was a huge achievement. I felt very encouraged and proud of my position. I had responsibility! It made me feel good inside. I was doing something worthwhile again and I could feel some of my confidence coming back.

My social worker had encouraged me to take the job. She seemed to believe in me and that helped too. She told me she had a wardrobe full of lovely clothes and she sorted some out for me so that I had something decent to wear to work. I felt she really cared because she did things for me that were beyond the call of duty. I thought a lot of her. She continued to take letters to the children and she told them that I loved them. That was brave of her, because she knew my mother hated me. I think she realized that the reason for my struggle had a lot to do with my relationship, or lack of it, with my mother.

One day I was working in the shop when my mother arrived with my children (she always seemed to find out what I was doing and where I was). It was the day before Mother's Day. Chay and Bonita waited outside while she came into the shop. I was standing by the till and I watched as she approached. She proceeded to empty the contents of her shopping bag onto the counter. 'I thought you would like to see what they've bought you for Mother's Day,' she said. Then she put the package back in her bag, left the shop, took Chay and Bonita by the hand and walked up the road with them.

I used to dread Mother's Day. I had good reason. The year before that incident my mother had phoned the social workers to suggest that it would be a good idea if I saw my children again. It must have appeared as though she was really trying to co-operate and be a peacemaker. She brought the children to my flat, and I had gone to a lot of trouble and prepared a party for them. Chay, Bonita and I played bob the apple in the bath. We got soaked and we giggled and laughed together. It was lovely.

After the tea party (I've still got the pictures my children drew that day) my mother went home and phoned the police. She told them that I'd tried to drown Chay. About two hours after she'd left, two policemen called at my flat and I was taken to the police station and questioned. Every time I got near, every time I got sober, every time I seemed to be making progress, something happened – or was made to happen – to stop me in my tracks.

The police rang my social worker and she came and talked to them. They were ready to charge me because I couldn't prove I didn't harm Chay. After all, I was the one with the bad track record. However, she sorted it out for me and no charges were pressed. I was very fortunate that I had that social worker, because I don't know what would have happened without her help.

After that I didn't see my mother for many months. I used to see my children, although they didn't know I was nearby. Their schools had been informed that if I showed up I would hurt them. So I couldn't meet them from school, or even be seen anywhere near the school grounds. I was very cautious because I was so frightened of doing anything that might hamper my chances of seeing them and having them with me again. But I did go and see them. I'd stand out of sight beyond the playground and watch them walking home. Sometimes I'd see them arriving at school. Sometimes I used to watch them at the shops.

It broke my heart that I couldn't even tell them I was there. I didn't know what they were thinking; they may have been afraid of me and I didn't want to frighten them. I also knew that it would cause a lot of trouble if I approached them. I asked my social worker if they could be moved into a children's home. At least then I'd be able to visit them legitimately.

However, I was told that for that to happen they'd have to be taken to court and made to stand in a witness box to answer questions. So I had to make a decision. What was best for them? I made what I thought was the best choice and decided it would be too harrowing for them. They should stay where they were. Maybe I chose the wrong way; I'll never know.

Time went on. I had my ups and downs, but each time I fell I got up again and tried to go straight. I was desperately unhappy and I was still cutting myself during bouts of despair. But at least I was earning a little bit of money. I even had a telephone! I'd never had one before.

One afternoon in 1985 I had a call from my social worker to tell me that someone from the social services office, my mother's social worker, would be phoning me shortly. She told me I had nothing to be afraid of and I was not to worry. So I put the phone down and it rang again more or less straight away. The man on the line told me that he was speaking on behalf of my mother. She'd been to see the social services to discuss Chay and Bonita's future happiness. He told me that she'd decided it wasn't fair that I wasn't seeing my children.

As I listened, I could hardly believe what I was hearing. My heart soared. He told me my mother now felt it was time that everything was put right. The children themselves wanted to see me. It was arranged that I would meet them at the social worker's office in Carshalton.

I put the phone down, stunned. I would see Chay and Bonita in three weeks' time. Three weeks! I hardly dared believe it! It had been months and months since we'd spent time together. I went into a frenzy of excitement. How can I begin to describe what those three weeks were like? How should I wear my hair? What should I wear? I was changing into this and changing into that, running round to Pam and asking her opinion. By the time those three weeks were over I was a nervous wreck, strung up with excitement. Was this the breakthrough I'd been hoping for?

It was arranged that I would see them at 3.30 in the afternoon. It was a beautiful summer day in early June. I arrived early, feeling happy but terrified. I was shown into a room, a small room, where five social workers were sitting with my children. I was invited to sit down with Chay and Bonita in front of me. All that morning I'd been rehearsing what I was going to say and when it came to it I couldn't utter a word. I think I just told them how beautiful they looked. I was crying with joy.

Then they each handed me a letter. As I opened the letters I saw they were both exactly the same. I slowly started to read, and I thought my eyes were playing tricks. I kept glancing up at the children's faces. They were looking at me intently. There was something wrong. There had to be a mistake. Was this some kind of cruel joke? I couldn't believe what I was reading: 'We hate you, we never want to see you again. Don't you ever upset our nanny again and here is your Christmas present back.' Then they handed me the Christmas presents back, still wrapped.

I couldn't stem the flood of tears. I was inconsolable. I walked straight out of the building and into the lake. The social workers ran after me, trying to say how sorry they were. They told me they'd had no idea what was in the letters. They hadn't known this was going to happen. I'm sure that was so, but I knew *why* it had happened: I was getting too well. My mother didn't want that.

I've since learnt that Chay and Bonita were made to copy those letters. Even at the time I knew they didn't mean what the letters said. I could see it in their eyes. The letters were the same, word for word. The only difference was in the name at the bottom. This happened in June. I was devastated by the discovery that they still hadn't unwrapped the Christmas presents I'd sent them six months before.

I went on the biggest drinking binge of my life and took another overdose. Once I was out of hospital I started cutting myself again. I don't remember much about that time. It's all lost in a fog of alcohol. I lost my flat. I lost my job. I just drank and drank and drank. I was picked up by any man who cared to have me. As long as he bought me a drink, I didn't care.

I started sleeping rough on the streets of Sutton. There was nowhere else to go. I went from bad to worse. I was eating out of dustbins and if I did get any money my mind immediately told me it was beer money. I never spent any money on food or clothes.

I lost contact with my social worker. She didn't know where I was. I didn't want to be found. I hated myself so much and was so full of guilt because of my children. It wasn't that I didn't care about them. I did, desperately, but after a blow like that I couldn't hold my life together any longer. I was worn out, and bereft of hope. I just wanted to die. All I possessed were the clothes I stood up in. I wore a pair of flip-flops on my feet. I didn't care what happened to me and found myself in some terrible situations.

One morning, as I told you at the beginning of the book, I woke up in a room with four Arab men. I didn't know who they were or where I was. I didn't even remember being taken there. I realized those men had made me very drunk and then taken full advantage of me to amuse and satisfy themselves. As I lay there, I saw them staring at me. But they'd had all they wanted and were already preparing to leave. For all I could do about it, they could have killed me. But I walked out of that dreadful room alive.

Another time I woke up to find my face had been badly scratched. As I came round I discovered I'd rolled down a railway embankment. I might have fallen from the road. Or did I jump out of a car? Or was I pushed out and left to roll down the embankment in the dark? I don't know what happened. Everything was just a blur. I didn't know how I got the bruises or marks I had. I could have landed on the railway tracks themselves without knowing a thing about it. I put my life in danger every day, but someone must have been looking after me.

I was filthy and smelly; people shunned me in the street. I didn't have any clean clothes to change into. I didn't wash and I was soaked in my own urine. You just lose control when you're really drunk; you wet yourself and mess yourself. I didn't care until it got to the stage when no man would buy me a drink in exchange for sex.

Then I really was on my own; and I felt completely alone, shut off from everybody. I was sleeping in doorways most nights. Sometimes I went up to where my old flat was because I still had a key to the cupboard by one of the swing doors outside it. Like an animal I could crawl into the cupboard where at least it was warm.

That Christmas of 1985, I was filtering through some rubbish bags, trying to keep a step ahead of the dustbin men, and I found half a turkey and six chocolate yoghurts! I thought that was wonderful. To me this was a feast and I ate the lot.

I was quite used to eating food from dustbins. I searched in them every day. On this particular day, because I didn't have any money at all to buy drink, I was suffering withdrawal symptoms. And the withdrawal symptoms from drink can be quite horrendous.

You shake, you sweat, you can't keep your legs still, you have panic attacks and you can go into fits, which I did a couple of times. You feel extra-sensitive and find everything more frightening than it really needs to be – even a pin dropping seems like a huge noise. You go into the DT's (delirium tremens), a form of delirium which brings terrifying delusions. Your body chemistry is all mixed up because of the destruction wreaked by the alcohol, and you just feel so ill.

But worse than all that is what is going on in your head: the shame. Oh, the shame when you're sobering up! It's worse than anything else. You just want to get drunk again so that you don't have to think about how ashamed you are. It's a vicious circle. In this state I'd drink anything. I didn't care. Anything I could get. It was literally a case of beggars can't be choosers.

I remember the first time I really looked at myself then. I was covered in flea bites. I had lice on my body and in my hair. My fingernails and toenails hadn't been cut for months and they were black and cracked. My hair was so matted that I had to cut it off – all of it because I couldn't get a comb through it and it was so full of nits. I had sores all over my body. I was painfully thin. I had so many cuts, bruises and abrasions, and I didn't know where they came from.

I was obviously undernourished. So much alcohol destroys the vitamins in the body. As I was not eating properly I became very ill, caused not just by abuse and neglect, but also by the constant infections from eating soiled food. My whole body was so abused and wrecked that there wasn't one bit of it that I was proud of. I'd also been cutting myself and these wounds had become infected because I hadn't been looking after them.

Over Christmas 1985, when I was sleeping rough, the weather was particularly cold and I didn't have a coat. I slept in what I stood up in along with lots of newspapers. I was cold, but I don't think I noticed it that much at the time. I was dead in my head and in my heart. I'd given up. I had nothing left to live for. I just wanted to die, but somehow I kept waking up. This was the lowest point in my life.

After Christmas, I still had no money to buy a drink. I was walking the streets one day and as I shuffled past the Salvation Army hall in Sutton, I saw that there was a jumble sale going on. I hadn't had a drink for a couple of days and my hands were shaking. But I thought how good it would be if I could just get a cup of tea – if I could hold it and keep it in the cup. The worst thing about the DT's is that by the time you get the cup to your mouth it's empty because you're shaking so much. (And you can guarantee that if you go into a detoxification unit they always give you peas, and a fork to eat them with ... it's a standing joke among alcoholics!)

I loved jumble sales; I still do. I'm teased now because I still carry a black bag around with me to collect things in! I can really understand those homeless people who push trolleys around with them. Those few pieces of personal belongings really become important. All I had in my black binliner then were a few bits and pieces and a few photographs of my children.

Drawn by that jumble sale and the possibility of tea, I stopped. It was snowing and I was cold and tired, so I went into the Salvation Army hall. Little did I realize it then, but within an hour my life was to change for ever.

eLEVEN

My friend

I sat at a table by myself with a cup of tea. I didn't want anyone to come and talk to me. They wouldn't have done anyway, I thought – I smelt so awful. There were a few other dossers there, men mainly. I recognized them, as our paths often crossed, but I had no reason to communicate with them. We had nothing to offer each other except shared experiences.

I don't remember buying it – I had no money, after all – but on the way out I somehow acquired a book. Outside I sat down on a bench clutching my black bin liner; I never let it out of my sight. It was still snowing. Having been in a warm room for a time, the bitterly cold wind stung my face and hands. Then I looked down and realized I was holding this book. As I looked at it more closely, I saw that it was a little Catholic missal, a Book of Common Prayer.

My hands were very cold and the snow was making them wet, so I turned with my back to the wind to try and protect the thin paper pages. I was fumbling, trying to open the book. I don't think anybody had read that book for years, and the pages were difficult to prise apart. I wasn't thinking about anything in particular, apart from a vague curiosity about this little book. I was very cold. I was sober; I hadn't had any money for days to buy drink. I also knew I had a lung infection and this was making me feel very unwell.

Every movement was an effort, I had so little energy. When I eventually managed to open the book, a piece of paper fluttered to the ground and fell face down into the snow. For a moment I lost sight of it against the white background of the freshly fallen snow. Painstakingly I bent down and gently searched with my hands until I felt it, limp and already wet. I picked it up and turned it over. To my surprise I found myself looking into a black-and-white picture of the face of Jesus.

It was at that moment my whole life changed. It sounds so ridiculous after all that I've told you and after all the failed attempts with people who'd tried to help me in the past. But as I sat on that seat my life changed, just like that.

Oh, I knew Jesus, I remembered his picture from my childhood. I'd loved Jesus when I was little. After all, I'd been brought up a Catholic and went to a church where I'd looked at pictures of him every Sunday. I'd seen statues of him in the convent. I knew what he looked like! But this picture was different. As I gazed at his face he seemed to be speaking to me.

The picture showed his face and a little bit of the top part of him. His eyes were looking down. His face was long and thin and there was a very big crown of thorns on his head, with blood running down his face. And as I looked at his face I felt so broken. It was as though I was being drawn into the picture, not just looking at it from a distance like an observer in an art gallery. Something was going on inside me.

As I looked at his face I thought Jesus looked in a worse state than me. I felt there was an empathy between us. I think I felt compassion for him, which was a strange emotion for me to feel towards anybody else at that time. A lot of people, of course, would say I had the DT's – it was all a delusion. Well, if that was so they were the best DT's I ever had because they saved my life! But I know different. It wasn't a delusion.

As I was looking at the picture somebody spoke to me – but nobody was near me, although I looked round to see. I didn't know anything then about the gifts of the Holy Spirit or that God could talk to you. I remembered him as a fearsome God. I remembered that I used to love Jesus but became very angry with him over my father's bizarre behaviour and the things he did to us.

But I did hear a voice, as I sat there in the snow. And the voice said to me, 'If you drink again you will make him cry.' I don't really know why or how, but I knew then that it was God talking to me. As I looked at that picture I understood that I *could* make him cry. I'd never thought before that he would bother to cry over me.

I stared at the picture and knew it was true. It was his pain. It was the look on his face. It was the sheer sadness of his expression. I actually turned round then because I thought somebody was sitting next to me, but there was nobody there. I'm sure that some people will think after reading my story so far that I was imagining things, hallucinating even. But I knew it was God's voice. I've never forgotten it.

I've since learnt that Jesus has the knack of touching the one part he knows no other person can reach; like that Heineken advert, he touches the parts no other spirit can reach. He knew that drink was my vulnerable point. He knew that there wasn't one other person who would have cried for me that day. He knew that no one else cared about me. And he was telling me that he loved me so much that if I picked up another drink it would break his heart. That really meant so much to me. And I know it was God speaking to me because that experience, that meeting with God, changed my life.

Then something else wonderful happened. It's important to remember here that for a long time I hadn't been physically or emotionally close to anybody. From June 1985 until now, early 1986, I'd lived alone on the streets of Sutton. I'd become a filthy drunk nobody wished to associate with. I was an embarrassment to my family and if my children could have seen me then they would certainly have been ashamed and frightened of me.

As I sat on that bench, I had a clear sensation of somebody coming and sitting down next to me, and I distinctly heard the word 'friend'. In that moment the King of Kings and Lord of Lords had come down from his throne in heaven and sat down next to this old, dirty, smelly tart sitting on a park bench. That hadn't put him off. As I thought about it and gazed at the picture still in my hand, I saw that he'd left his throne, left everything that was up there – all the riches, the angels, the people singing to him, everything that he'd attained, to come and sit next to me. And I was just a whore. I'd never felt so loved in all my life.

I suddenly felt a surge of emotion rush through me like an electric charge. This in itself was a strange, unfamiliar sensation. For months, my emotions had been numbed, I hadn't felt anything. But somebody, something, had reached out to me and found me even though I'd sunk so low.

As a child, I used to imagine Jesus with a white beard and a friendly face, with long arms that went on for ever. That day it was as though Jesus reached down into the depths and found me, then put his arms round and round and round me. He just coiled himself around me until I was in a cocoon. And then he gently pulled me out of that hole. It was as though the rest of the world couldn't see me any more – I was invisible to them. I was just his, he made me his, he hid me in him, and I knew I was hidden. I didn't know then the words in the Bible, 'You are hidden with Christ in God,' (Colossians 3:3) but that was my experience.

I don't know how long I sat there because I didn't have a watch. I think it was quite a long time, probably a couple of hours. As I sat staring at this picture with all these thoughts going on inside my mind, something else occurred to me. For the first time in I don't know how long, I suddenly realized I didn't feel lonely any more. But what was even better, I no longer felt afraid .

Until then there had never been a time in my life when I'd been free from fear *and* sober. I drank because I was afraid. I didn't stand up to anyone because I was afraid. I hated myself because I was afraid. I couldn't look after my children because I was afraid. Fear had wrecked my life. Fear had been a part of me for as long as I could remember. Maybe it had been a part of me since before I was born, brought to me in the womb through the family lines, because everyone in my family was afraid.

But now I wasn't afraid. I felt as though I could take on the world. I firmly believed that what I'd found wasn't going to leave me; it wasn't going to play a dirty trick on me.

The feeling was so intense that I didn't dare come out of it for a moment. I didn't want it to go away. As I concentrated on Jesus' face I knew that I would die for that man. I knew there was nothing I wouldn't do for him, and without question he was real, without question he had come into my life. I knew I was going to dedicate the rest of my life to him. I knew it all in that moment. But I can't tell you how I came to know so much in that short time.

After a while I actually started talking to the picture. By now anyone passing by would have thought, what a dirty old drunk! I didn't care what they thought, I was so happy. I'd just fallen in love. Exactly as I'd done before when I fell in love, I could put down the bottle straight away. I'd always needed a crutch, whether it was a person, a tablet, an injection or a drink. I hadn't been able to stand on my own even after that first panic attack just after Bonita was born all those years ago. So now I knew I didn't need the drink any more – I didn't need anything because I'd found someone I knew wasn't going to leave me. Yes, I'd fallen in love looking at that picture, but this time it was a marriage made in heaven. This time things were going to work out differently.

Then I felt something move beside me, and it was as though the person next to me actually came and moved to be *inside* me. And I felt loved, I just felt so loved, from the inside out! All this had happened as the result of me looking at the picture. God had intervened in my life. He'd come to find me when I hadn't even asked him. I think he saved my life just in time, because I was very ill, and my body surely couldn't have taken much more punishment.

I suppose I was surprised that this had happened to me, but I didn't question it. I didn't say to Jesus, 'How do I know you're real?' I just didn't want to let him go! I didn't want to break it. I didn't want the feeling to disappear. Not that there was any magic or fairytale drama attached to this. It wasn't like a Barbara Cartland story. A tall dark stranger riding a white horse didn't suddenly gallop up to me, whisk me up into his arms, take me to his castle, bathe me in a bubble bath, dry me in fluffy towels, give me fresh clothes to wear and tell me I was really a princess after all!

No. It all happened very quietly. But just as a seed germinates in the soil out of sight and in secret, so I believed something was reborn inside me that day.

Eventually I got up from that bench and walked off. I was still dressed in filthy old clothes and I still smelt as I had done before. I still carried my little friends, the lice. Nothing outwardly spectacular had happened. As I shuffled up the road nobody said to me, 'God has just told me to give you a hot meal and a room for the night.' Nothing like that happened at all. I just walked off up the road with my picture in my pocket. But it seemed as if someone was holding my hand. I could feel it.

I didn't know where I was going, but I kept hold of his hand and I wasn't afraid. That night I slept rough as usual, but I had my picture in my pocket and I had my friend by my side. I knew he was there and nothing could have shaken me from that certainty. After all, he wasn't just next to me, he was in me. And still I wasn't afraid.

Something had changed in my thinking. I was no longer the same person who had gone into that Salvation Army jumble sale wanting to die. I had found that picture, and my life had been changed as never before. For the first time ever I knew for sure that God existed, that Jesus loved me and that he'd come to live with me.

tWELVE

Steps towards new life

Over the next couple of days the change in my thinking started to affect me outwardly. I was stirred by this newfound feeling of peace and confidence. I'd never felt like this before. It had to be from God. There was no other way I could have got rid of the fear I'd experienced for so long, especially without drink or drugs!

I decided to go to the social security office. I surprised myself because I was able to talk quite calmly and coherently and explain my needs. The next thing I knew, I was walking out of there with some money in my pocket so that I could buy some basic necessities, and the one-bedroom flat I had previously rented in Sutton was vacant so I was able to move back in immediately. I was thrilled.

The next thing I did was visit the job centre, looking for work. Then I went to the careers office and enquired about training opportunities so that I could learn how to use word processors and computers.

I was amazed at myself! I could never have behaved like this before, nor talked so confidently to anyone without first having a drink. I would have been too scared. But I found I now had an overwhelming desire to get my life in order. What amazed me even more was that I made the right decisions about who to go and see – especially when I consider what state my mind had been in only a short time before.

Alcoholism inflicts such a lot of damage on the body as well as the mind, and I'd been an alcoholic for a long time. They tell you in the Alcoholics Anonymous meetings that if you're lucky you die and if you're unlucky you live, and the last stage of alcoholism is Korsakoff's Syndrome. (Sergei Korsakoff was a Russian neuropsychiatrist.) When you've reached the stage of having Korsakoff's your thinking has become really muddled. When you try to read the newspaper, for example, you read the first word and by the time you get to the second you've forgotten the first. But you know you've forgotten it. It's a living hell.

I wasn't quite at the stage of having Korsakoff's Syndrome, but obviously my thinking power and my decision-making abilities had been impaired. Added to that, I hadn't planned or thought about doing anything by myself – or even for myself – for such a long time. But all of a sudden I was making the right decisions and I was knocking on the right doors.

I can only describe it this way: I had a living relationship with Jesus. I'd found a friend and I was asking his opinion. I didn't know how to pray 'properly', but all day I was saying things like, 'Well, what shall we do now, Lord?' And I'd feel the reply in my heart: 'I think it's best we go down to the job centre.' I'd know where to go because he told me!

When I went along to the social services office and spoke to the social workers, they were obviously impressed by my improvement and change in attitude. I was delighted to have my old flat back. It gave me a sense of picking up where I'd left off, rather like seeing an old friend again after a long absence. After all this time, I had a room of my own once again.

I was really starting to get myself sorted out. Things I needed kept falling into my lap, which only served to encourage me all the more! People started to give me things. I joined an evening class to learn how to use a word processor. At the college I met a young woman and, although I was friendly towards her, I was careful not to tell her too much about my history. But one day she turned round and said, 'Could you do with a bed and some curtains?'

It was a constant source of amazement and encouragement to find I was continually meeting all the right people. Somehow I was in the right places at the right times. I know now that God was guiding me. I understand it all now, but then it was just one surprise after another.

To save money I went along to one of the hand-out places where they give you a few clothes. This meant that with the grant from the social services, I was able to buy a few other essentials and pay for my word processing course.

I also registered at the local health centre. The doctor put me on a course of vitamin injections, but other than that there was very little he needed to do for me. My body was healing itself. I told him a little about my history, because at that stage he didn't have my medical records. But when I went back for the next appointment he did have my notes on his desk, a thick bundle!

'Oh no,' I thought, 'he's not going to want to know me now.' But he was so nice; he was really kind to me. I'll never forget him saying to me, 'I can't believe from reading your medical records and looking at you that you're the same person.' He asked me what had made me suddenly pull myself together. I told him my story, and he laughed!

He gave me some antibiotics for the cuts that were still healing, and the vitamin injections helped me to feel better too. It should really have taken me a long time to recover from the battering that I'd had. Not only had I been sleeping rough, I'd also sustained quite a few injuries and both my eyes were black. Much of the time I hadn't known what had happened to me so I couldn't tell the doctor – he had to draw his own conclusions.

After just two weeks on the word processing course, armed with my new-found confidence, I walked into a secretarial agency and said, 'I can use a word processor. Can I have a job please?' I'd only had two lessons! The lady in the agency took me seriously, so I must have started to look quite convincing.

While I'd been sleeping rough on the streets for the past seven months I'd become used to people looking at me in disgust. In fact, because of the shame I felt, I'd long since stopped looking people in the eye. But now all that had changed. As I gradually began to lift my eyes again, I found people were taking notice of me and even asking my opinion. I must have appeared 'normal' to them. I was no longer treated as a non-person. I thought about this a lot, and decided it had to be something in my spirit; it had to be what shone out of my eyes that convinced people I was trustworthy. People were now talking to me as if they wanted to know what I had to say.

The receptionist in the agency handed me an application form and I nearly died. I read it slowly, my eyes moving down the page from one question to the next, and as my eyes moved downwards so did my spirits. I realized I had nothing to offer but several years' 'experience' in Netherne Hospital! For references I only had magistrates, doctors, policemen, psychiatrists and social workers. I didn't know how to fill the form in.

As I stood there clutching the form I prayed, and heard my friend's voice. He just said, 'Temp.' So that is what I did. I gave the form back and said, 'I think I would like to temp for a little while.' By the end of the week the agency had found me a temporary position at a place called Distillers. It's funny, isn't it, that I, an alcoholic, should be offered a job working at a place with a name like that!

I'd made some friends at the evening class, including a girl called Aylsher. But I was very jealous about the time I spent with my Lord. I didn't really want anybody else getting in the way of my friendship with him. I was really happy in this relationship. I talked to him from the minute I got up in the morning to the minute I went to bed. It was an undiluted time with Jesus and my love for him grew and grew.

At first I didn't join a church. I did go along once to the Sutton Christian Fellowship. Strangely enough, it was a spiritualist who took me. She invited me round to her house for a cup of tea one day. When I arrived she said, 'I see a man standing next to you with a red train.' 'Oh no!' I thought... Then she said to me, 'I'm going along to this new place tonight, and they have prayer for healing.' I think she thought it was going to be a spiritualist meeting! So that is how we both ended up at the Sutton Christian Fellowship.

I sat at the back in a corner and I loved it. Especially the singing – I'd never heard anything like it. It was so beautiful. I felt quite at home and relaxed in that church. Then the most surprising thing happened. The preacher came down off the stage and walked towards the back of the church to where I was sitting. He came straight over to me and, taking me by the hand, led me up to the front.

For the first time since I'd known Jesus, my heart started to race and I was really nervous. Then the preacher put his hand on my head and told me that the Lord was bringing me out from the corner and he was going to cause me to shine among the nations. He said these and other words over me that I can't remember any more, and then he prayed for me. After that he walked back up onto the platform and I walked back to my seat and cried.

I never did go back to that church, but I think God used my spiritualist friend to take me there that night, because it really encouraged me. It showed me that I hadn't just been imagining that Jesus was with me. If the preacher saw it too, then it must be true!

At this time I still didn't have a Bible. All I had was the Catholic missal I'd picked up at the Salvation Army jumble sale. I read it from cover to cover and the words in it came alive to me. On one page I found a hymn about a wandering sheep. The sheep wandered so far from home that it lost its way and lay exhausted, cut, bruised and bleeding. The animal was on the verge of dying when Jesus found that sheep and bathed her and washed all the blood away. Then he gently lifted her onto his shoulders and took her back to be with the rest of the flock.

Every time I read that hymn I broke down and cried, because that was also my story. Jesus had come looking for me when I was lost, and now he was nursing me and caring for my wounds. As I read that hymn again and again, I knew that was what he was also doing in my heart. All the people, all the hurt, all the distress, all the sexual abuse, all the degradation, all the pain surrounding my relationship with my mother, the rapes, and the loss of the children – he was taking all of it and he was mending me. And not only was he mending me, he was doing it so skilfully, restoring me to be the person he created.

In just a short while my life had changed dramatically. Once again I found the energy that gave me the determination to begin the fight to get my children back. I never thought I'd feel that way again. I'd had so many disappointments. But as the days went by, I became confident that this time Jesus would help me.

My job as a temp at Distillers went well, and before long they offered me a permanent job. Then, after just two months, they promoted me! I was earning a lot of money by my standards. I bought myself some smart clothes and got to work improving my little flat.

If anyone else had seen it they would have laughed. I bought some shiny satin, peach-coloured material for the curtains and hung some ivory-coloured net curtains with big bows at the window. Round my bed I draped swathes of white material to create what I can now only describe as a giant meringue!

Every week after I'd been paid, I either bought myself something to wear or something for the flat. I didn't spend any money on drink and so this was my reward. I was building a home for my children. I was trying to create a place that would impress them. But, of course, after being out of touch for so many years I didn't really have much idea about current design trends! That didn't matter. It gave me something to occupy my spare time, as well as giving me hope that each passing day was a day nearer a reunion with Chay and Bonita.

There were lots of times when I was tempted to drink, and occasionally that still happens to me today. What usually triggered me then was seeing my mother with my children. This happened often because we lived so close to each other. If she saw me she would never speak and that was always very hurtful, especially as she could see I was smart and clean and looking after myself again.

Then the temptation to have a drink would come. It was as though a glass of wine was passed under my nose and I could smell it. But as soon as the temptation entered my mind all I had to say was 'Lord', and it was gone. I learnt to do this gradually, but as I got better at it I could see the temptation heading for me and I would say 'Lord' before it got a hold on me. I was growing!

For the next two and a half years I carried the picture of Jesus everywhere I went. At times life was a real struggle. There were some nights when I was very lonely, not lonely for a man but longing to hold my children. And the more sober I became the more urgent I felt about getting them back. I desperately wanted to see them and I really wanted them to see that I was getting well. But I couldn't work out in my mind how this would happen. I still felt that all the odds were stacked against me.

But I wasn't ready to give in. I continued to walk with the picture in my pocket and every day I only had to look at it if I felt insecure or if I wanted a drink. I looked at that face and I couldn't make him cry, I just couldn't.

I started going to jumble sales on a Saturday and because I didn't earn that much money I'd allow myself just £10 to spend on clothes. Then I'd take them home and wash and iron them, and if necessary mend them or sew the odd button on. The next day I'd put them in an old pushchair that I'd bought, and take them to a local car boot sale where I'd set up a stall and sell them. I was regularly making a weekly profit of between £70 and £80. Not a bad return on £10! I saved every penny of this money, so that when I had Chay and Bonita back I could afford to rent a house big enough for the three of us.

This particular car boot sale was held at the back of the local pub. Before long I got to know the other stall holders. They were a friendly group of people, and I was soon accepted and doing quite well. My sister Pam and her husband knew I was there because they lived just over the road. I often called in on them on the way home.

One Sunday I had a shock. The door opened and I saw my mother coming into the area where the stalls were. She came and stood right in front of me, looking at the clothes I had for sale. Bonita was with her.

Bonita was 13 years old then, and I thought she looked lovely. I didn't know what to do. I was so stunned. I hadn't been that close to my daughter for years. If I'd put out my hand I could have touched her. My mind was racing. What should I do? Would I frighten her if I said 'Hello'?

My mother stayed in front of me, pretending to look at the clothes. It was torture. I couldn't stay silent. Eventually I said, 'Hello, Bonita.'

Immediately my mother grabbed my daughter and pushed her at me, screaming at the top of her voice, 'There's your f***ing mother who f***ing doesn't love you, who's never f***ing fed you!' She grabbed Bonita by the arm and threw her at me again and again, yelling at her, 'If you f***ing want her you f***ing have her!'

Bonita was hysterical and I said, 'Bonita, Bonita, don't cry. I won't hurt you, I love you. I won't hurt you.' But she was absolutely terrified of me.

My mother grabbed her by the arm and shouted out to everybody, 'She's a whore and she's my daughter, but I'm telling you now I don't have a daughter!' Then she walked out and left me standing there, with everybody looking at me in stunned silence.

I grabbed hold of my picture. I pulled it out of my pocket, held it in both hands and just looked at it. I was terribly upset. Then the door opened again and in ran

Tom, my brother-in-law, with his friend. Within seconds they had carried me out with my clothes and pram. They put me in a van and drove me round to Pam's house. There they calmed me down and took care of me until I'd got over the immediate shock and distress.

This sort of thing happened quite regularly for the next couple of years. Each time I was terribly shaken, but not once did I reach for the bottle. Instead I reached for the picture of Jesus, and he never ever let me down. What did seem to be happening, however, was that my mother had started to show her real self up in front of people who knew her. Until then all they'd heard about was this terrible daughter who'd beaten her up, hit her and knifed her, and who wanted to kill her own children. But all of a sudden people were starting to see that I wasn't like that.

God taught me to use these situations to learn how to trust him. Every time I pulled that picture out of my pocket and asked God to help me, he turned up and he helped – in fact, he was there all the time. I began to have such a confidence in him that he *became* my confidence. After that I didn't feel afraid, nor could I be made to feel afraid by the sudden shock of these incidents.

I became even more determined to get my children back. It was as though I had tunnel vision and they were at the end of the tunnel. God encouraged me not to look to the left or the right, but to keep going, heading for my goal.

tHIRTEEN

Opening doors

One day at work somebody tapped me on the shoulder while I was in the canteen eating my lunch. 'Don't I know you?' this woman said to me. I must admit, this was the one thing I most dreaded. After all, I'd been a prostitute, and had spent months on the streets, drunk. What if this was someone I'd insulted when I was drunk, or what if they'd seen me do something shameful that I couldn't remember? It was my biggest worry of all, and here was someone asking me this question at work!

My immediate thoughts were, 'I've blown it, I'll have to leave this place and start all over again.' But then another thought ran through my head: 'No, don't be silly, Jesus is here.' I calmed down. But who was she? 'Don't I know you?' she'd asked me.

I said, 'No, no, I don't think you do!' I didn't recognize this person at all.

'But I'm your cousin, Susan,' she said to me.

'Who?' I was baffled.

'Susan,' she said, 'Susan Braithwaite, don't you remember me?' We hadn't seen each other for 22 years and yet she recognized me! She belonged to my father's side of the family. Twenty-two years before there had been a major row between our two families and they had never met or spoken since, but now here was my cousin Susan and she remembered me.

I don't know how she recognized me, especially when you consider the life I'd led. I was overwhelmed with happiness as we hugged each other. Briefly she told me about her life. She had her own sad story to tell. One of her children had just died. She had another little girl, but her marriage had recently broken up. She told me all about her family and what had happened to them over the years. She suggested that we meet that evening after work, and she would take me to her home in Redhill to meet her family.

For the rest of the day I was in a whirl. I couldn't get over what was happening in my life. I seemed to be going from one surprise to the next. Susan had phoned her mother to tell her about our meeting, and when we arrived at the house I was given a very warm welcome and introduced to relatives I scarcely knew about! It was extraordinary that after a break of 22 years, that night I met 22 cousins, aunts and uncles!

I hadn't been a welcome part of a family for years. All of a sudden I was being accepted into a family that I'd long forgotten about and certainly never expected to see again. And what's more they were interested and pleased to see me. They all wanted to hear what had happened to me and sat quietly as I recounted my story, occasionally inter-rupting to say how sorry they were. 'If we'd known,' they said, 'you could have stayed here, we would have looked after your children, we would have helped you.' They'd had no idea what had been going on in the other half of the family and were shocked and upset to hear of the troubles.

I got home to my flat very late that night, tired but elated. What was going on? After a few hours of fitful sleep (I was too excited to sleep deeply) I went to work the next day as usual. Susan was there and we both felt overwhelmed by our meeting the day before. My relatives phoned me regularly after that and I often visited my aunt and uncle.

One evening, I'd just returned home after visiting them, when the voice I knew said to me, 'Put the keys through the door and walk out now.' The voice was the same one which had said to me on the bench, 'If you drink again you will make him cry.' But what was he asking me to do now? I wasn't sure I understood.

I looked at the 'meringue' over my bed and said, 'But the children are only up the road here. I can't go away because I'm near them here, and what if they come and look for me?'

I was puzzled, but I phoned my sister and said, 'Pam, I think I've got to go.' I explained what I thought I had to do. She pleaded with me not to leave, but the feeling inside me was so strong. I said goodbye to her, put the phone down, and walked out of my flat.

I took a train to Redhill and went to my aunt and uncle's house once more. I told them that I'd walked out of my flat and didn't intend going back. They were very supportive and understanding and drove me back to collect a few clothes. After that I slept on their sofa for six weeks. I found a new job, a well-paid secretarial post with Foxbury Vauxhall in Redhill. I never went back to my flat after that. I didn't even miss it. I believed I'd done the right thing, even though I didn't know what the future held.

I'd only been with my aunt for a couple of days when she said to me, 'Angie, it's time you were born again.' She told me how she and my uncle and various other relatives had become Christians a short while before. I had no idea! The only one who wasn't 'born again' was my cousin Susan.

My aunt invited me to go along with them to their church. I went and met the pastor – the man who is now my husband. I was introduced to him but he didn't shake my hand, which I thought was strange at the time. He told me much later that as he reached out his hand to shake mine, he withdrew it quickly because he caught a glimpse of all the pain inside me and he knew that he would frighten me. I don't know whether he would have frightened me or not, but I was immediately impressed by this man.

I soon felt at home among the people at the church. They made me very welcome and I enjoyed going to the services on Sunday as well as meetings during the week for prayer and Bible study.

I settled into the area very quickly and before long I was invited to share a house with another girl who worked at Foxbury. So I moved out of my aunt and uncle's house and started to settle down again.

I loved the church Fellowship. And I learnt to pray in a group. This was a new experience for me. For a while it felt strange sharing my friend Jesus with other people; but as I heard their stories I realized I wasn't the only person he'd helped recently. They were keen to tell other people about their faith, so I learnt to do the same and it wasn't long before I was walking up to people in the street, complete strangers, and saying, 'Can I pray for you?' It was wonderful. I'd say to people I met, 'You look so unhappy, let me pray for you,' and they did! I was bursting to tell my story and share with other people what Jesus had done for me.

I was also hungry to learn more about God, and it was at this time that I bought my first Bible. I bought myself a copy of the New International Version and a couple of marker pens. Every spare moment I had I spent with Jesus, praying and reading my Bible. I still enjoyed his company more than anybody else's and the more I got to know him, the better and stronger I felt.

Things were going well for me. But I was concerned at being so far away from my Chay and Bonita. Not that Redhill is so far from Sutton, but it was the furthest I'd ever been from them. Gradually, though, I was beginning to trust that God had everything in hand. I trusted him implicitly and I could see that good things were happening in my life. After all, he'd moved me to Redhill, and I could see that there must be a reason for it, so I started to relax and wait.

I was surrounded by people who loved me for who I was. I had a good job and I was being paid quite well. My goal was still to secure the children. Everything I did was motivated with the thought that when I find them, when I see them, I'm going to be sober and well. I became obsessed with getting stronger and stronger. I kept telling myself I had to do better – in fact I almost caused myself never to sleep. Maybe I was setting myself impossible targets, but this time I was determined I wasn't going to blow it again. I'd come so close so many times before. This time things *had* to have a better ending.

I felt I had to prove that I'd changed for good. If my mother should ever see me I had to be exactly the opposite of what she'd seen before. I had to get as high as I could and be as well as I could, live in the best house I could and never have a dish not washed up or the floor not cleaned. I think I overdid things here, because I did make myself quite ill with too much effort! But in going all out to get my children back, I was instinctively building my defences against attack.

It took me a while to realize that I didn't have to do that any more, because now I had Jesus they had to get through him before they got to me. Old habits die hard, and I was having to learn that now I had Jesus to help me, *he* would be the one who would do the fighting for me. I didn't have to depend on my own wits any more. All I had to do was give him my problems and pain, and my desire to see my children again, and let him sort it out. How often we strive to make things happen when all we need to do is ask God to help us, and then wait and watch for him to act.

One night in August 1987, not long after I'd joined the Fellowship, Pastor David came to see me. We talked and he asked me to tell him my story. After listening for a long time he gently said, 'God is the God of loneliness, God is a God of love and God is a God of reconciliation. Do you believe this?'

'All I know is, he'll cry if I drink again,' I replied.

So David took me through the Bible and showed me verses to reassure me that the things he said were not his own ideals and empty hopes, but rather God's promises to his children. Then he prayed with me. He said, 'Let's pray now for God to give you your children back.' I almost didn't want to pray this, just in case it didn't happen, because then I'd have to blame God for not keeping his promises. It seemed too direct, too black and white. But we did pray, and then David left.

After he'd gone, I thought about his words and they rang true to me. I found myself wanting to believe them. I went upstairs, opened my Bible and started to read: 'Knock and the door will be opened to you' (Matthew 7:7).

Today I describe myself quite often as a 'Jack Russell Christian': I grab a verse and shake it to death and I don't let go. My jaws are locked around it and I just hang onto it until I've got everything out of it. Well, as I read this verse it leapt off the page at me.

I'd gone to bed at about eleven o'clock and knew I had to leave for work at seven in the morning, but I knelt by my bed and prayed right through the night until it was time to go to work. And I prayed with my arm up in the air, banging for hours on a door I couldn't see. I didn't just pray the words, I did what they said.

As I knocked on that door I soon understood why I'd never directly asked God for the children back before. It was because I was so ashamed. Then, before I knew it, I was weeping and confessing everything to God and telling him all about the children. I remember saying to him, 'I'm so sorry for what I've done to them.' I begged him to forgive me for all the wrong things I'd done and I promised him that if he gave me Chay and Bonita back I'd teach them all about him.

I confessed everything that night, and drew up my agreements with God before having a shower and leaving for work. Fortunately I was able to come home early because we worked a flexitime system. I was exhausted after praying and crying all night.

As I opened the front door of our house at about half past four that afternoon, I could hear the phone ringing. I picked it up and it was Pam. 'Angie,' she said to me, 'you'd better sit down.'

I thought one of the kids had been hurt. 'What's happened? Tell me, what's happened?' I cried.

'Are you sitting down?' she said.

'Yes.'

'Angie,' she said, 'Chay is here.' It was scarcely 10 hours since I'd finished praying! 'He wants to see you,' Pam told me. 'Can you come round to our house quickly?'

fOURTEEN

Chay and David

Pam had kept in touch with Chay and Bonita for me over the years and she'd given me news about them during the time I was unable to see them. It had been difficult for her. She couldn't tell them she'd seen me, as this would have caused even more upset within the family. Sometimes, though, she'd given them presents from me but pretended they were from her. To this day I don't know how she managed to keep our meetings a secret from the rest of the family; but she did and I'll always be grateful to her for her loyalty, love and support.

But Chay realized somehow that Pam knew where I was. That night he'd gone to my sister's house and pleaded with her to phone me. By this time he was 16 years old, legally free to decide for himself who he wanted to live with, and he wanted to speak to me now!

I could tell from Pam's voice that there was a sense of urgency. I *had* to get round there as fast as I could. Who would take me? I was so tired from spending the previous night praying, but now a surge of adrenalin rushed through me and I sprang into action. I rang for a taxi and paced impatiently up and down until it came. I felt overwhelmed about Chay, but there was no time to stop and think, to take in the moment – I had to get moving!

The taxi arrived and I jumped in before it had properly ground to a halt. All the way to Pam's house I prayed out loud! That poor taxi driver – I'm surprised he didn't take me straight to Netherne Hospital. 'Please God, put the right words in my mouth,' I prayed. 'Please God, don't let my brothers find him before I get there. Oh God, please don't let him leave. Oh God, please don't let my mum find him. Oh God, please.'

It was dangerous for Chay to have done this and it was brave of Pam to let him stay with her and then ring me. After all these years, was this the moment I'd been living for? Surely nothing would go wrong now? He *wants* to see me ... I had to keep reminding myself. 'Hurry, hurry!' I urged the driver.

At last we arrived at Pam's. I ran up the stairs, burst through the door, and there was Chay.

When I'd last held him he'd been a little boy. Now here he was, 16 years old and six foot three inches tall. It hadn't occurred to me that he would be so big! I was dumbstruck and couldn't speak to him. Chay got up from the sofa, walked over to me and threw his arms round me. 'Oh mum,' he said, 'it must have been so hard for you.' He'd been through hell for years, yet in an instant he forgave me.

We clung to each other for several minutes. It was a dream come true for me. I cuddled him and held him and stroked his face; I couldn't let go of him! And he kept telling me he loved me.

But we had to think quickly. Chay had run away from my mother's house and he didn't want to go back. He'd come to find me, he said, and now he was never going to leave me again. But he was so frightened of my brothers coming to find him. He even carried a knife in his pocket, and a spoon which he'd sharpened on one side like a razor. He'd learnt how to fight and look after himself. (Within three months he'd thrown these weapons out and carried a Bible instead. I kept my promise to God.)

Where were we to go that night? I rang Pastor David and told him what had happened. After all, it was his prayer that had been answered! 'I'm in trouble here,' I told him. 'I can't take Chay back to my place because I only have one room.' David told me to bring him over to their house. By the time we got there, another friend had heard about Chay coming to find me and she was waiting at David's house to take us to her own home in Reigate, where Chay could have a room of his own.

Much later that night, after talking and talking, we decided we just had to snatch a few hours sleep. It had been an exhausting 24 hours. I found I couldn't sleep, however. I crept into Chay's room and sat by his bed for the rest of the night listening to him breathe. I was so scared that if I went away he'd stop. I did that night after night. Every time he went out of the house I was on my knees, praying. 'Oh God, please don't let my brothers find him; let him be all right.' He was the most prayed-for kid!

Chay had recently left school and found himself a casual job. He never went back to my mother's house. We lay on the floor for hours in the evenings reading the Bible together. Before long Chay became a Christian and my pastor baptized him.

We rang the social services and the social worker who was originally involved in arranging for Chay to be looked after by my mother came to visit us. He sat on the sofa and listened quietly while we told him our story. He told me how sorry he was about everything that had happened to me and the children during the past 10 years.

Then Chay asked to speak to him alone, so I left the room for a few minutes. When they called me back in, I could see Chay had been crying and the social worker looked concerned and upset. He just said again that he was so very, very sorry. Chay never told me about their conversation, except to say that he had it in his heart that no child should be parted from his mum in the way he had been.

I believe that when I came to the Lord it broke the power of the generational sin in our family, and my children were set free too. We had freed ourselves from the trap of years and years of dysfunctional family life, which had simply been passed down through whole generations without any means of escape. And I believe that when Chay became a Christian he was cut off from the effects of his past and so was able to look back on his life without any bitterness.

He wanted to tell all the young people he met who were also from unhappy families: look what's happened to me, I've got my mum back. He used to bring people home if they had alcoholic mothers or fathers; he'd even bring the alcoholics home as well! He'd walk through the door and say, 'I'm just going upstairs to get changed, mum. Tell him how to get sober!' And somebody I'd never met before would walk into the kitchen. Chay had such faith in me that I could do the job in the time it took him to change! He was so proud of me, and he told everybody about me.

His one sadness was that he'd had to leave Bonita at home with my mother. But he'd had no choice. Bonita was only 14 then. He knew he couldn't take her away from her legal guardian at that age unless he had a place for her to live. So he had to leave first to find a home for both of them, otherwise she would simply have been found and sent straight back. That would have been even worse for her because she would have been punished by my mother and brothers for running away. Chay had worked all that out and considered the risks before putting his plan into action.

For the time being the two of us settled down with my friend Jan in her house in Reigate. We went about our various jobs during the day and met in the evening, often going to the church for prayer meetings or Bible studies. Life started to settle down and Chay and I were so happy to be reunited. We were just longing for Bonita to join us.

A few months later, however, our happiness was shattered. Our pastor's wife, Pat, died in a traffic accident leaving five little children.

I loved Pat. It was Pat who had opened her door to Chay and me that first evening when it looked as if we had nowhere to go, even though she already had 22 people living in her house! She was the kind of person who would try and do anything for anybody. Pat was an Irish lady who could love the most difficult person, who could argue furiously, and who occasionally became extremely angry. She was full of sudden enthusiasms. If she suddenly fell in love with pot plants, the house would be filled with them within a week. If she went off them, they were gone in two seconds. She was a passionate woman.

She was generous, too, but she was generous to the point that she wore herself into the ground. Pat tried to be a good pastor's wife, but people still criticized her. I can't help feeling that if people had given her more support she would still be alive today. As it was, in a fit of exhausted despair and a flash of anger, a minor incident led to her death.

Her husband, David, had given up his previous job to run the church, so Pat became the breadwinner and had a full-time job as a nurse working night duty at a local hospital. She was still trying to give out help to others during the day, but I don't think she had anything left, she was so tired.

On the day of the accident she and David were giving a birthday party barbecue for Luke, one of their five children. David was cooking the food when it was noticed that a beefburger was not quite cooked enough and Pat took it out of the child's hand. A row followed and David – I know what he's like, I've been married to him for 11 years: he won't row – walked away and got into the car. As he was reversing out of the drive, Pat opened the back door and jumped in. She really wanted him to have a row with her, but he wouldn't.

They had travelled about two miles down the road when Pat said, 'If you don't stop the car I'm going to jump out.' Then she did open the car door. David immediately looked in his mirror and saw her lying in the road. She died the next day in the Atkinson Morley Hospital. It was a tragic accident.

The whole church was called to a meeting the night that Pat died. I was there with Chay. An accusation was made against David and I suddenly felt afraid. At first I didn't understand what was wrong, but then I realized quite clearly that Jesus wasn't there. For the first time since becoming a Christian I felt Jesus wasn't with me.

I went outside and said, 'Where are you, Lord?'

'I am where the children are crying,' came the reply.

I didn't go back into that church meeting. I got straight onto a bus and went to David's house. Chay came with me. We went to see if we could do anything to help. We found the house in a mess. The children were distraught, and David was just sitting there in shock, drinking a bottle of claret, oblivious to their needs, unable to help them. All traces of family routine had broken down. They were all making themselves something to eat as and when they were hungry. David was just numb, and not in condition to look after the children on his own. Chay and I were glad that we'd been alerted to their need.

A few days later there was another shock. Somebody made an anonymous phone call to the police and accused David of having a sexual relationship with one of his daughters. David was arrested and taken to the police station. He was put in a cell for the night and his clothes were taken away from him. His daughter was also taken from the house and questioned. They proved pretty quickly that it was a false accusation and apologies were made, but an accusation like that always has to be investigated. It was enormously distressing for all concerned, especially as the family was already struggling to come to terms with Pat's death.

I started going to David's house every day after I'd finished work. I'd do the washing and generally help to keep the house clean and tidy. I carried on like this for about nine months, by which time the children would get very upset when I left to go back to my own home, especially Katy and Damian, the youngest children. Some nights I slept with them in their bedroom because they were so distraught. It didn't take long before this caused gossip, but I didn't care. I knew I wasn't doing anything wrong and I just couldn't leave them like that, I just couldn't.

During this time, I fell more and more in love with the whole family and so did Chay. On his way home from work each evening he'd buy a big bag of penny sweets. The shopkeeper must have dreaded the sight of him because it took so long to count them all out! But he'd come home with his pockets full of sweets, take charge of the children and watch television with them. He loved them and they loved him. They were like his brothers and sisters and he spoiled them.

I may have been organizing the household very efficiently, but by now my emotions were in turmoil. I'd walk up the road saying, 'Oh God, what's going on?' I knew I was in love with David and I just kept falling more and more in love with him – but I couldn't say anything to him. How could I when the whole family was still in pain from Pat's death? Chay knew – he knew straight away. 'Mum,' he said, 'you're in love,' and that made me feel guilty because he'd only just got me back. But I needn't have worried about Chay's feelings being hurt. 'It's all right,' he told me, 'don't worry, I love him too.'

I couldn't tell if David was in love with me. He was still very introverted, still sitting there crying a lot. He'd weep for hours and hours, or sit slumped, eating a curry and drinking claret, although he'd never been a drinking man until then. He had no will to do anything and he very rarely got dressed. He hadn't just lost his wife, he'd also lost his job as pastor of the church: he'd lost his whole life in one blow and everyone he thought he could trust had deserted him. People he'd loved and helped were pointing the finger at him. Well, I'd experienced that for years and I wasn't going to do that to him. I knew what it was like to be on that side of the table.

All this time I kept my job on, but Chay and I moved to a flat in Horley so we could be nearer to David and the children. That way we could stay with them a little longer each night, but it was still getting to be quite an endless toil of rushing to work and rushing home to help out and get everything done. It was far from plain sailing. Of those five children, one had cerebral palsy, another was profoundly deaf. They had all lost their mother. When I thought of the mess my life had been in just a short time before, I was amazed at God. Who would have thought that I could help anyone?

Sometimes I'd look at Chay and wonder what he was thinking. Was he really happy? We didn't have that much time to ourselves any more, and we'd been together such a short time. He came out to the kitchen one day and we were sitting there on our own when he said to me, 'Mum, come on, let me get you out of this. I'll look after you. You don't really need this.' I just cried and cried. Then, as we were talking, Katy came into the kitchen. She slipped her hand into Chay's and he looked at me without saying anything more. I knew then that he didn't want to go anywhere else, whatever he might say about taking me away. He'd fallen in love with them too.

About nine months after we started helping David and his children, I was sitting and praying about how I felt and thinking that I'd really have to start easing myself out of the situation. David came in and we sat in the kitchen chatting. After a while Luke came into the room. He would have been 10 years old then. Luke is profoundly deaf and there are no grey areas when you're deaf, every-thing is black and white – he'd never hear our small talk and all the innuendoes of everyday chit-chat. He always went straight to the point.

So that evening he came into the kitchen, walked straight over to his father and picked up David's left hand. David had taken to wearing his wedding ring on his little finger and Luke pulled it off. He walked over to me and put the ring on my wedding finger. Then, turning to his father, he said, 'You know, she is my mummy now.' And with that he walked out of the room.

I didn't know what to say. I just sat there flabber-gasted. Then David said, 'I didn't know how to tell you how I felt!'

Luke came back a little while later and asked, 'Are you going to get married now?'

'Yes,' said David.

He was all right from that moment on. He stopped drinking claret, stopped eating curries, and started to get himself back in order. He had something to live for again. It was as though he'd just woken up from a long dream. As Luke had said in his own very direct way, 'How long are you going to sit there? Can't you see what God is giving you?' So just as I was praying and planning to ease my way out of the situation, everything seemed to fall into place and I stayed where I was!

I'm sometimes asked how, after all I've suffered at the hands of men, I could trust my emotions enough to fall in love again, let alone consider getting married. But I just couldn't help it. I'd never known anyone like David before. He was so different.

I'd never known anybody love God the way David loved him. I'd never seen a man be so hurt at the hands of other people. This man had loved and trusted people and they had kicked him in the teeth. That I could identify with. We shared a mutual understanding and experience in that area. And I'd finally met a man for whom I had immense respect, especially for the way he conducted himself throughout the time before we were married.

There was just one problem, however: I'd never divorced my first husband, Dick, whom I hadn't seen for 16 years. I struggled with this question of divorce because I wanted to do everything right biblically. The process took a long time and we had to wait nearly two years before we could be married.

Chay was very excited about the wedding. We were to be married in the June of 1989 and he was going to give me away. In the meantime we all lived together. That way it was easier to look after the children. I slept in an upstairs room with Katy and Damian, while Chay slept downstairs with Joey and Luke. Also in the house were some other people we were caring for. It was very busy!

By then Chay had a job working for the East Surrey Hospital. He was the warehouse man in charge of uniforms, dressings, and so on – in fact everything that had to be supplied to the hospital. His job was to make sure the warehouse was kept well stocked and to reorder as items ran out.

We spent our second Christmas together and Chay went back to work two days after the Christmas festivities had finished. There were still six months to go before the wedding. I saw him off to work that morning. He took a whole Black Forest gateau with him for his lunch and I'd made him some beef sandwiches. 'You're one in a million, mum!' he said to me as he left. I'm sure it was only because of the Black Forest gateau! I watched him go, thinking how much I loved my son.

I wondered sometimes if he minded sharing me with all the other children. But he didn't. Instead he asked me, 'Do you mind sharing me with them?' He was lovely. And he loved God so much. He lived to evangelize. He'd been to a couple of John Wimber conferences where his enthusiasm to share his faith had been set on fire.

He'd changed so much in the short time we'd been together. When I first brought him back to live with me, he had a knife and a sharpened spoon in his pocket. He'd been involved with a gang in Mitcham who were quite ruthless and violent. He'd had quite a lot to do with spiritualism too, but within a few weeks he was lying on the floor reading the Bible with me. After that he didn't take the knife with him when he went out – he took pockets full of tracts instead.

I went out evangelizing on the streets with him one day before that Christmas and watched as one chap ran off up the road because he didn't want to listen to him. Chay ran up the road after him. I think the man thought he was going to be mugged, because Chay was so tall! Well, Chay caught up with that man and pinned him against the wall, and I'll never forget what he said: 'You could be dead tomorrow, so you need to listen to what I'm telling you.'

But Chay was dead before that man was.

fIFTEEN

Death blows

We had such a short time together, Chay and I – just 18 months. When we were together in the evenings we enjoyed each other's company and chatted for hours. We were both hungry to know what the other had been through during the 10 years we'd been apart. We became good friends and very much at ease with each other. This was a constant source of amazement to me. I kept expecting Chay to show flashes of anger or disappointment at the unhappiness I'd caused him and Bonita. I thought he'd ask me a lot of painful questions. Every day at the beginning I waited for him to say, 'Why, mum? Why did you do it?' But not Chay: he didn't want to hurt me and add to the guilt that I already felt so acutely.

He told me he'd spent the past 10 years waiting to be 16 years old, because then he was going to come and find me. From the moment we were parted he'd decided that eventually he was going to look after me. We'd been extremely close when he was very young and it was a bond that never broke, despite everything that had happened. Chay had been six when I was taken to Holloway prison, old enough to remember his early life with me. But

Bonita was two years younger, and her memories of me must quite naturally have faded more quickly.

Chay described to me how, when he was alone in bed at night, he secretly thought about his plans, counting off the years and months still to go before he reached 16. He'd dream about coming to look for me. Maybe that had been his way of dealing with the pain of separation.

As I listened to him, I remembered how I had pined for my children in prison. I thought of my friend Margaret who'd attempted suicide because she couldn't bear being parted from her children. Listening to Chay made me realize that he'd gone through his own deep valley of fear and uncertainty, not knowing when or if he was going to see his mother again. What had he told his friends at school? I wondered.

To hear him describe how he'd hidden those plans and secrets in his heart often moved me to tears. And worse than that, I felt the heavy weight of guilt, because it was me who had caused his pain. He'd done nothing wrong; he and Bonita were the unfortunate victims of my failed relationships, my agoraphobia, my drug addiction and alcoholism. If only it had been a bad dream and I could have woken and found that it wasn't like that at all! Whilst I'd been full of feelings of despair and self-pity, experiencing the frustration of never knowing if I was ever going to be believed and helped, Chay and Bonita were serving their own sentence. Talking with Chay then, I had to face the stark reality of their suffering too.

How could he forgive me so willingly? I didn't deserve his love and generosity; he had every reason to despise me. But he didn't, and I gratefully accepted his love. It was like a soothing oil being gently poured into the deep wounds of my heart and mind. He brought such peace and reassurance into my life. I loved him so much; I was amazed that it was possible to love somebody as much as I loved Chay during those 18 months we were together!

His ambition had always been to provide a place for the three of us to live together again as a family. He understood why he had to wait until he was 16 to make any move. He told me he'd often been tempted to run away and take Bonita with him. But the thought of being caught and returned to live with my mother and brothers frightened him too much. For a child he was very mature in his thinking – he instinctively knew it would only make life much worse for them all.

He didn't tell me much about what actually happened to him during the years we'd spent apart. I've found out since.

He wanted us to start a new life together in every respect. When he became a Christian his own new life just took off! He became a fearless evangelist. He met an evangelist at Spring Harvest called Lindsey Hamon who became a role model for him. Lindsey had undertaken several long walks of witness carrying a wooden cross and Chay was overwhelmed by this man and his faith – so overwhelmed that he invited, or rather cajoled, him to come and have a meal with us. Poor Lindsey arrived to be confronted by this huge family of strangers, not quite knowing why he was there. But he had a gentle and humorous personality and we quickly relaxed and enjoyed each other's company. Little did I realize then what that first meeting was going to lead to for me.

Chay decided he wanted to do what Lindsey had done: he wanted to build a cross and walk with it round the whole coast of Britain. Over the next few weeks he discussed his ideas with Lindsey, who was enthusiastic and encouraged him to make his plans and go ahead.

Chay had applied, and been accepted, to join the Fire Brigade after his eighteenth birthday. It had always been his ambition to be a fireman. In fact, as a child he'd had a rather unhealthy fascination with fire. He once admitted to me that while he'd been living with my mother, he sometimes stole personal items belonging to her and burnt them. He'd done this on several occasions, usually after she'd said something bad about me. I think he felt that joining the Fire Brigade would channel those tendencies into something positive!

It was arranged that he would resign from his job at the hospital at the end of the year, spend the next three months walking round the entire coastline of Great Britain with the wooden cross he'd made, and then he would join the Fire Brigade in March 1989, just after his eighteenth birthday.

He wasn't just going to walk with the cross for the sake of it. He intended to say to every child he met on the streets: 'Have you got a problem at home? Do your parents not love you? Does your mum drink? Because if you have, I know a man who can help you.' He'd drawn up his plans and built his cross, but he died before he could start the walk.

With just a few days still to go at the hospital before he left, he went back to work on 28 December, with his Black Forest gateau and beef sandwiches, and I'd watched him go without a qualm. At about 11 o'clock in the morning two policemen arrived at the house. I was outside tidying up the front garden.

'Do you know where Mrs Boorer lives?' they asked me.

'I'm Mrs Boorer,' I said.

'Does Chay Boorer live here?'

'Yes.'

'Have you got somebody with you?' said one policeman.

By this time I was starting to get frightened. I wanted them to tell me what was wrong, but I feared they had something awful to tell me. 'Where is my son?' I said to them. 'Tell me where my son is.'

Then one of them said, 'He's dead, love.'

'Dead?' I said. 'No, it's a mistake. He's gone to work. Where is he? What's happened?'

But they just repeated, 'He's dead, love; he's dead, he's dead.'

I don't remember any more. David was upstairs asleep in bed because he'd taken a job as a night porter to earn a little money and had been out all night. I ran up the stairs screaming. David heard the commotion and was on the landing by the time I'd reached the top of the stairs. He went downstairs and the policemen told him what had happened. They asked us to go with them to the hospital to identify Chay.

By this time some more policemen had arrived and we were taken in a police car to Crawley Hospital. We were asked to take a seat in the waiting area of the casualty department. I'd given Chay a signet ring for his seventeenth birthday. A doctor wearing a green gown came out to see us and he was holding this ring. He put it in David's hand. Then I realized it was true. As I looked at that ring I knew it had been taken from Chay's hand and he was dead.

'Would you come with me?' said the doctor. We walked in a silent procession down a long corridor. I remember there were pipes running along the walls, and I thought it would never end. Why is it that morgues always seem to be in the bowels of the earth?

By the time we were halfway down this corridor, my own doctor, who is a Christian, had caught up with us.

We stopped at a door. Someone opened it and we were ushered into a cold, white room. There in the middle was a table with a body covered in a shroud. An orderly pulled back the cover to reveal Chay's face.

'Is this your son?' they asked me. I looked at him. There was a policeman guarding him, and it all seemed so unreal. I walked over to Chay.

All the way down the corridor I'd been praying, 'In the name of Jesus, get up, in the name of Jesus get up.' I'd made up my mind that I was going to say to Chay, 'Get up in the name of Jesus and breathe.'

But when I stood close to him he looked so white. I put out my hand and stroked his face. He felt so cold. I climbed up onto the table and lay down beside him. I couldn't tell him to come back. I looked at his face and for the first time in his life he was in a place where he was at peace. He was with Jesus. I tried to say, 'Get up in the name of Jesus.' But what came out was, 'Thank you for giving him to me, God, and I give him back to you.'

I didn't want to say that. I wanted to tell him to get up, but I couldn't. I sat with him for a while. He still had the clothes on that I'd bought him for Christmas. They had emptied all his pockets and given me his belongings, including a tract he'd been carrying around with him, I still have it. It had a picture of a tombstone on the front and the words, 'I expected this, but not yet.' Inside it said, 'If you need any further information, contact Chay.' He'd been handing these out to people on the streets just that morning.

They told me how the accident had happened. Chay had climbed up onto the platform of a forklift truck driven by a friend, just to say hello. But as he'd stepped up his foot had knocked his friend's foot and moved the control that makes the truck go forwards or backwards. It jumped violently backwards, and Chay was thrown off and crushed against a wall.

It was odd, I reflected. David and I had been joined by death – first the death of his wife, and now the death of my son. When I was a little girl I'd lived just a couple of houses away from David, although I hadn't known it. And when my marriage to Dick had started to break down, when I was living in Brixton, David had lived just down the road from me, although I hadn't known that either. It wasn't until all those years later that we met, when we needed each other most.

I felt I had nothing left to live for when Chay died. I thought I would die too. At first I couldn't believe it. God had given him back to me and everything had been so wonderful. I remembered the first few nights after Chay and I had been reunited, when I sat by his bed and listened to him breathe. I couldn't believe then that God had given him back to me. It took me a long time to relax and not worry about him every time he went out.

People would say, 'Trust God, he hasn't given him back just to take him away again.' But I thought even then that was the most stupid thing anyone can ever say, because who knows what's going to happen? I think we should spend every day giving all the love we can. Who can tell how long any of us have left to live?

I didn't have Chay for long, just 18 months, but I showed him as much love as I could in that short time. I didn't take one day for granted and I'm glad of that now.

People have asked me whether the shock of Chay's death caused my faith in God to waver. It didn't, not for one minute. I just fell into God. I had nothing else. He was there and I dived in. I was in a terrible state for weeks, but

I remember that the first night after Chay died I fell asleep praying and I woke up the next morning still on my knees.

I didn't understand why this accident had happened, but I knew it wasn't God's fault. All I could do was run to the only friend I knew, the one who had never let me down, and say to him, 'Please hold me.' He'd held me since he'd first found me and had never put me down.

Even before Chay died, I'd started to realize that there had to be a reason why God had spared my life. There had been so many occasions when I could easily have died or been killed. I think it started to occur to me as I was falling in love with David. I had Chay back and people were starting to depend on me.

For years I'd let people down. I'd been drunk. I'd been stoned. I'd always been in a mess. I'd been unreliable. But now I got up every morning to see those five little faces at the breakfast table, some mornings crying for their mum, other mornings happy and chirpy. Some nights I'd tuck them up crying, too, but other nights I'd tuck them up giggling. They needed me, and Chay had needed me too.

In the 18 months with Chay I'd regained a great deal of courage and strength. He'd helped me, there was no doubt about it. Through Chay, God had given me hope, because I discovered that during the long years we'd been parted, he'd never forgotten me. That's forgiveness. That's the story of the cross. It all comes down to someone forgiving you.

After Chay died, David and I weren't sure whether to go ahead with our wedding, which we'd planned for June. But Chay had been so excited about this wedding. I was going to walk down the aisle on his arm and he was going to give me away. He'd loved and respected David so much, and I know he'd loved the kids as well. So we decided we would go ahead.

In recent months David had been looking unwell and was in considerable pain. In fact, that Christmas Chay had given David all his bonus money, £80, so that he could go to an osteopath and receive some treatment for the pain in his neck.

After Chay's funeral, and despite the increased pain that David was experiencing, we started to organize our wedding in a way that included Chay. We were married 'legally' in Reigate registry office one day, and the next day were married 'properly' (the day I considered to be our wedding day) in Horley Church.

The reception was held at home. I prepared it all myself and we served the food in Chay's room just to make him as big a part of the celebration as we possibly could. We ordered dozens of red roses and had a picture of Chay enlarged and put in a china frame that we hung above the wedding cake.

Dozens of friends came to our reception. Then, after a long but happy day, David and I drove wearily off to Norfolk to spend our honeymoon in a cottage some friends had arranged for us to enjoy for two weeks.

David collapsed for the first time on our wedding night. We'd only just arrived at the cottage. He was in so much pain. Somebody who didn't know I was an alcoholic had left out two bottles of champagne to greet us. Desperate for something to help him, I said to David, 'Well, I hope you're ready for this, because I'm going to teach you how to drink now!' It was all I had to take him away from the pain. In half an hour he drank both bottles of champagne. I carried him up the stairs to the bedroom, where he passed out and slept until the next morning, when I managed to find a doctor.

During the first couple of months after the wedding, David was in constant pain and regularly collapsed. He was finally diagnosed as having cancer. There was a tumour as big as a grapefruit at the top of his spine.

sIXTEEN

God's arms are long enough

Early married life was not at all what we were expecting it to be. David soon became very ill and three months after our wedding he was no longer even able to walk. It was to be another two and a half years before he walked again. Within the space of nine months we had buried Chay, got married, and now my husband was paralysed and fighting for his life.

I think David was more devastated than I was. The one thing he dreaded in all the world had now happened to him. For years he had harboured a fear of one day being paralysed and having to be dependent on another human being for everything, with all the loss of personal privacy that entailed. I knew he had this horror because he'd shared it with me from the time we started to become close.

Once the full extent of the tumour was realized, a way had to be found of eradicating it. David had a type of cancer that couldn't be operated on. So it had to be treated using chemotherapy, and later with radiotherapy. It took months. But that was good news, because when he was first admitted to hospital he was given only three days to live!

When we were first told the prognosis we felt absolutely desperate. David had gone into hospital thinking he had a slipped disc. But an X-ray showed otherwise. We were immediately told that the situation was very serious. The tumour was inoperable and probably fatal. David, in particular, felt that death had become a personal enemy which just wouldn't leave us alone. In a matter of weeks his blushing bride had become a potentially grieving widow.

He wanted to tell me the news himself and persuaded a ward sister to let us use a private room so that we could smoke. David hadn't smoked for years, but he didn't think he could get through this without one, and he didn't think I could either!

After he'd told me I didn't really know what to say. I asked him if there was anything he'd like me to do and he said he'd like me to wash his hair. So, without more words passing between us, I calmly washed his hair before leaving to catch the bus home. I'll never forget that day.

For the past few months we'd been attending a Vineyard church in south-west London. John Mumford was our pastor and became a very close friend. On the day Chay was killed, by the time we returned home after identifying his body in the morgue, John had arrived to be with us. I don't know who told him or how he got there so quickly, but we were glad of his company then.

And he was there again when I received the news that David was probably going to die. We met on the old stone steps outside the hospital. 'Ang,' he said, 'we've got to stop meeting like this!' We sat down together and he said, 'I don't know how to pray.'

I loved him for saying that – he's so honest. He was just the same when Chay died. He didn't come out with a lot of words, he just sat there and said to me, 'I don't know what to say to you.' That was real to me, because that was how I felt; I could cope with that. But now here we were again, and this time it was David. As we sat together on those stone steps and prayed, I asked God for a Golden Wedding!

At first David felt sure he was going to die and I think he was mentally preparing himself for that. He suddenly found he was afraid of death once it was staring him in the face. But we were able to talk and pray about it, and it wasn't long before that fear went.

Then he used to phone me sometimes during the night and beg me to let him die. He'd say, 'You've got to let me go. For God's sake, give me permission to die. I've got to go.'

That was the worst part of the illness. I could handle everything else. I'd say, 'No, I'm not going to let you go.' And he'd reply, 'Please, I can't take any more.' I didn't want him to die, but I didn't want him to suffer either and the emotional trauma of that for both of us was enormous. I started to feel guilty. Was I being selfish?

I tried to persuade myself that he'd be better off dead and I should let him go in peace. But I couldn't. I loved him too much and wouldn't entertain the idea of being parted from him. So death was not an option. Rather, I found I had the faith to pray for his complete healing. Once I'd reached that point and come to the unshakeable conclusion that such a thing was possible, I found a huge strength returning to my mind and body. I was able to get on with life and do all that was required calmly and confidently.

But I knew it was hard for David. He was lying helpless at the very time he wanted to be a support to me. Despite having recently lost Chay, I was now trying to be the new mum to David's five children, while he could do nothing. He was completely paralysed and I quickly had to learn how to care for him, including his most basic needs: manual bowel evacuation, cutting his toe nails, washing his legs, and cleaning his groin to guard against infection. It was round-the-clock care and I stopped work to look after him.

I also knew that the children were frightened. They didn't want to lose their dad – we were agreed on that! I was functioning totally on the strength that God was giving me each day. There was nobody else to help me. Once again we'd become very isolated as a family. David's illness seemed to open up some old wounds and I was once more on the receiving end of some painful accusations from other Christians.

I remember hearing Fiona Castle being asked on the radio what she'd found the hardest thing to cope with after Roy's death, and she replied that it was the anonymous letters she'd received. I thought then: If I could meet you now, Fiona, I'd hug you for saying that. Not many people would admit they receive anonymous letters, which by their very nature are always unkind and meant to wound. But such letters were one of the most painful things I had to endure at that time, and I couldn't share my distress about them with David because he had enough to put up with already.

I'd dread the postman coming up the drive. Every day he'd deliver three or four letters, all accusing me of being the whore who'd married their pastor. God had already killed my son, they suggested. When was I going to learn that David would die too unless I left and moved out of the neighbourhood? What made matters worse was that these letters were often full of Scripture as well as hate, and that I found very hard to take.

Despite all this, our days did start to settle into a routine. Every morning, after taking the children to school, I'd catch a bus to the hospital and give David a bed bath. The hospital was a number of miles away and the journey took three hours each way. I'd just get back to Horley in time to collect the children from school in the afternoon.

They were always anxious to hear news of David and I had to reassure them that he'd had a good day and was getting better and would soon be home. They clung to me after school. They were worried about their dad and I desperately wanted to give them the reassurance they needed. It wasn't that long ago that they'd lost their mum, and only a few months since Chay had died. They'd adored him too.

Every day I marvelled that God trusted me with these broken children to look after. Not only were two of them severely handicapped, but they'd gone through all the emotions of bereavement twice in quick succession. Who else but God would have chosen the drunk on the bench to take care of them?

People will tell you you're no use. But that's a lie because *you* are the very one God will pick. He will use everything you have learnt in your pain and degradation. He will turn you around and treat you like a king or queen and use you to help other people. Why? Because you have suffered, you have compassion.

There is no such thing as being written off. I want to say to the world – it doesn't matter how low you fall, God's arms can reach you.

During this time, rather than crumbling inside like I used to, I was discovering more and more potential within myself. I wasn't reaching for a drink, I wasn't even tempted! No, I had to get up in the morning and make sure the children were all right. They needed me. David also depended on me to visit him in hospital and bath him and be with him for a while. I knew he lived for my visits.

It was a frenetic lifestyle, travelling to and fro, making sure I was back to pick the children up on time. But I was never late, not once. I felt so encouraged because I could never have coped with this level of responsibility before. Every day I just marvelled that God would even consider using me. It's strange to say it, but in the middle of so much that was painful, I felt so happy! I don't think the social workers would have picked me to look after those five children, but God had.

So this was a very special time for me. I matured in those weeks in areas where I hadn't developed before. God treated me gently, though – he knew I was damaged. When I looked at those five children, I thought how awesome my situation had become. I'd lost my whole family. I'd thrown it all away. I had no reason for anyone to trust me with five children. Joey had cerebral palsy; Luke was profoundly deaf. Suddenly David was out of the picture and I was on my own with them. Yet God was saying to me, 'I trust you.'

I couldn't understand this! I was so frightened that I'd do something wrong or omit to do something that I drew up a daily job list. I felt, after he'd given me this opportunity, that I couldn't let God down. If somebody knocked at the door I wanted the place to look exactly right – it had to be perfect, there couldn't be a hair out of place. So I scheduled my time to the minute: 7.00 a.m., get up, do the washing, do this, do that, dig the garden; 4.00 p.m., cook the dinner, bath the children, do the washing; and then at 11.00 p.m., long after they'd all gone to bed, I'd paint the hall, stairs and banisters!

I didn't feel tired, I was elated! I must have been living on adrenaline. Little by little, I was achieving things I never thought I could do. I even set about reorganizing the house. The kitchen was a mess and in need of a face lift, so I ripped the existing cupboards out, bought some wood and started to build some new cupboards.

I was so glad that Jesus was a carpenter, because he sat there in the kitchen with me and I asked him what to do next. I talked to him and said, 'What do I do now?' And he told me how to do it! The ideas just flowed into my mind. I designed and measured, sawed and screwed, sanded and painted, and gradually I put the fitted kitchen together.

I couldn't believe I was doing these things. God had given me a second chance, but I had to learn. And as I learnt and trusted him, I could feel myself changing.

One day I asked God, 'Why me? I've failed at everything. I was such a mess. How can you trust me?' And he reminded me of an old film about Thomas Alva Edison, the American who invented the electric light bulb, starring Spencer Tracey. Edison wanted to patent his light bulb and he was working in a basement room with a group of his scientists. Also in the room was a little boy, with trousers just below his knees, and he idolized Edison. He was watching as Edison tried to get the light bulb to work.

They had many failures, but finally they got the light to stay in the light bulb. Then Edison turned round and he gave this young boy the light bulb and told him to carry it upstairs and take it to the patent office. Maybe because Edison had once been a newsboy on the railway, he saw himself in this young lad. The child's face shone: Edison had spoken to *him*! He was so excited. But as he ran upstairs he tripped and dropped the light bulb, which broke into a thousand pieces.

As I watched the replay of this film in my mind, I saw the child sobbing with embarrassment as the scientists had to get back to work and make another light bulb. Finally, after several more attempts, they succeeded. Edison took it in his hands, walked straight over to the boy and told him to take it upstairs.

All the scientists said, 'Don't give it to him, he'll drop it.' But Edison replied, 'He's the only one here that I know *won't* drop it.' And I think God went to all that trouble to give the same message to me. I'd made so many horrendous blunders in my life, committed so many mistakes, but when I asked God to come and help me, he not only gave me a fresh start, he recreated everything I'd failed at and this time he walked through it with me. I wasn't going to drop the precious gift this time around. Sometimes I was frightened I would fail. But God has never once let me down.

By marrying David I had, of course, become a stepmother, and everyone knows this can lead to difficulties. When I first started to get involved with the family, Louise, David's eldest daughter, really resented me. I suppose it was her way of being loyal to her mother. I could see what was happening: her mum had just died, she was 18 years old and felt grown up, she was very beautiful but very insecure at the same time.

I think it would be fair to say that the relationship between Louise and her mother had been a little bit distant just before Pat died. I think when that happens and someone dies it's natural to build a false aura about them, where even the warts become beauty spots.

So Louise was hurting and frightened. Part of her wanted to assume her mother's responsibilities, but at the same time she wanted to be free to go out. She wanted clothes and all the other things that go with being a girl of 18. Louise and I had to work at our relationship and sometimes the tension would mount. On some occasions she'd stand outside the house and swear and shout. Or she'd collect the children from school before me and then I wouldn't know where they were.

I said to God one day, 'Look, this is all very well, but I keep holding out my hand and Louise keeps biting it. What am I going to do?'

'Keep holding out your hand,' he said to me, 'and when she eats up to your shoulder she'll be close enough to kiss.' I thought that was wonderful advice.

She did keep biting, but in the end she did get close enough to kiss. She came in one day and just put her arms around me and gave me a kiss on the cheek. 'I'm really sorry,' she said. Today we have a good relationship and we're very close. She's my staunchest ally. She's always there, no matter what's wrong. Louise is a diamond, and once again I proved that God's word never fails.

One day I was at the hospital visiting David. As usual the journey had taken me three hours and I didn't have long with him before I had to leave and get back to meet the children. While I was there a nurse approached me to say that one of David's doctors wanted to talk to me. They were considering allowing David home to carry on his treatment and they needed to show me how to give him his injections.

No sooner said than done – they promptly fetched some needles and syringes and started showing me, very slowly and deliberately, how to give a mainline injection. I could hardly keep a straight face. There was I, an ex-drug addict, being shown how to give a mainline injection as if I'd never even seen a syringe before!

My surprise and amusement didn't end there, because then they asked me to go to the pharmacy and collect David's prescription. They were planning to send him home the next day. Later that afternoon I travelled home on the bus with two bags of diamorphine, a box of needles, a box of syringes and a 'sharps box' (for the used needles)! I sat on the bus thinking, 'I don't believe this.' If I'd met a policeman who knew my history he would never have believed my explanation. But to me, God was saying once again, 'I trust you.'

The hospital wanted to make sure I was completely happy and confident about giving David his injections and offered to arrange for a nurse to come to the house for the first few days to help me. David told them quite candidly, 'No, it's all right. My wife used to be a junkie. She knows what she's doing!'

Everything I'd done wrong, God was using to put things right. I've come to learn that life is empty without suffering. Suffering brings out so much beauty and helps so many people in ways you'd never imagine. I have a saying: 'Look how much muck it takes to grow a beautiful rose.' Without the muck you don't get the blooms – and you certainly don't get the perfume.

sEVENTEEN

Using the
years of pain

That incident helped to persuade me that not only was God telling me he trusted me, but other people were trusting me too. It took me a long time to get used to being treated like this. For so long nobody had listened to me, let alone had faith in me. I sometimes wondered how long it would last before they decided I wasn't reliable again.

Negative thoughts were never far away. Some days it was difficult convincing myself that I *had* changed and that I was able to achieve everything asked of me each day. I battled with self-doubt and a low self-esteem. Many a time I had a two-way conversation going on in my head:

'I can do all things through Christ who strengthens me.'

'Oh no you can't. Remember the time you blew it and bottled out?'

It was a great encouragement to discover that the Bible talks about 'renewing our minds', or changing our way of thinking about ourselves. For me this was a gradual process. I was learning all the time and it helped to reinforce my positive thinking when people treated me with respect. I'd become so used to being at best ignored and at worst abused.

After all, many a time I'd been tossed out of a car and left on the roadside. Such careless rejection had become a way of life. Instinctively I knew that every time I would be pushed away eventually, once I'd served my purpose. The degradation had got worse and worse as time went on. Now, when someone suddenly wanted to know my opinion on something, it took my breath away. People even opened doors for me now. That had never happened before.

When I was alone on the bus travelling to and from the hospital, I often thought about these differences. They puzzled me. I came to the conclusion that I must have changed outwardly as well as inwardly. If complete strangers were treating me with dignity, helping me when I had heavy shopping bags, saying good morning to me in the hospital, then I must appear friendly and approachable. But I was still Angie!

I think the change started as soon as Jesus came to live in me, that day I went to the Salvation Army jumble sale. As I pondered on the mystery of it all, I decided that my heart and emotions had been the first area to be touched. Then, as my mind cleared, I was able to think logically and start rebuilding my life again. When I'd visited my doctor he'd certainly been surprised that my body was healing itself so quickly after the battering it had taken.

After that, as I lifted my eyes and started looking at the world around me, I saw in other people's eyes my own experience being reflected back at me. I knew if they were hurting inside, I could see it in their eyes.

Those years of living off my wits meant that people couldn't easily fool me! In order to survive I'd become good at conning people, and alcoholics and drug addicts are notoriously good at manipulating both people and situations. That is how they live and get away with what they get away with. But even this aspect of my character has been wonderfully useful since I've become a Christian. Quite often I know what people are going to say before they open their mouths!

Just before David and I were married, it was as though God was telling me that I was not ever going to be able to settle down to quiet marital bliss! He had other plans, and wanted me to use the years of unhappiness I'd experienced to help other people. It was then that I had another surprise, another amazing indication that everything I'd been through could be turned round to positive use.

Gradually, various doctors in the Horley area who knew my history began phoning me to ask if I could help them with patients who were alcoholics. They told me how these patients were taking hours of their time and even then they didn't feel they were getting to the root of the problem and helping them effectively. One morning I had a call from a doctor friend to say that one of her patients, an alcoholic, had been admitted to Netherne Hospital. She was married with four children. Would I visit her and try to find out the real cause of her drinking?

Before going to the hospital, David and I drove round to the woman's house to meet her husband. As we walked through the front door and I looked at this man, my heart froze. I instinctively knew that he was using his wife's alcoholism for his own advantage. I felt he was encouraging her to drink by making sure there was always alcohol available, and then when she was inebriated he was selectively phoning a few sympathetic people asking for their help and advice.

Not realizing his deceitfulness, these people would come and see the dreadful state his wife was in, and agree with him that she was incapable of looking after their children and should be hospitalized. But his motives were entirely selfish – he had a lover and he wanted her to come and live with him, but first he had to get rid of his wife.

I challenged him immediately: 'Where have you put the drink?' But before he could open his mouth I walked straight over to it. I knew where he'd hidden the bottles, in a cupboard by the door, but only because that's where I would have put them.

Armed with the information we'd gained from visiting the husband, we drove to Netherne Hospital. This was the first time I'd been back. As we drove slowly up the long drive, the memories of that place flooded back into my mind. Seldom had I returned to that hospital voluntarily during my time as a patient!

David parked the car outside the main door and we walked silently in. My doctor friend had informed the receptionist that we were coming and we were told that Kate, the patient we'd come to visit, was 'in review'. The psychiatrists, social workers and other nursing staff were in a meeting to discuss her case. Knowing her GP had requested that we visit Kate, we were invited to join them.

It was all so familiar. Their chairs were positioned in a circle around Kate. They were talking about her and deciding if she should stay in hospital or be sent home. As was usual in these meetings, Kate's opinion was not sought. She'd only been admitted to Netherne that day, so this was her initial review.

I looked at Kate, this woman I'd never met. I couldn't see her face. She was sitting very still and gazing at the floor, and the long black hair falling over her shoulders concealed her expression. She looked such a mess.

I felt very self-conscious and certain that I was going to be recognized as a troublesome ex-patient. It was ironic: how many times had I been the person sitting in the middle being judged? Now here I was, a member of the jury in the very hospital where I'd been incarcerated for so many years!

But I was to be no mere observer. Suddenly one of the psychiatrists turned to me and said, 'What do you think? What's your opinion?' I could hardly believe my ears. Had they really asked me for my opinion?

For a moment I struggled in silence. What should I say? Had I read the situation correctly at the house? Did I know something nobody else knew, not even Kate? Could giving my opinion make any difference to her situation? What if I was wrong?

But I had nothing to lose. So I spoke up and told them exactly what I thought was going on between Kate and her husband. And they listened! Soon all eyes were on me. The puzzlement and concern that I'd read on their faces as they were discussing Kate's case turned into expressions of understanding as they began nodding their heads in agreement with my analysis of the situation.

To my utter surprise and delight we walked out of Netherne later that afternoon with Kate, and took her back to our home. My opinion had been valued to the extent that Kate was entrusted to us until her family situation could be sorted out. I was so thankful to God. Once again he was showing that he trusted me to help one of his children who was hurting so badly.

Kate was one of dozens of people that David and I have subsequently been able to care for and help on the road to recovery.

It wasn't long before I felt God was saying to me, 'I don't just trust you with five children, I'm going to trust you with thousands of suffering people.' All the loss and unhappiness that I'd experienced could be of use. I understood how an alcoholic felt, how a battered wife felt, or an abused child, a prisoner, a drug addict, or a homeless person. They didn't have to struggle to describe to me the predicament they were in – I knew!

But did I want to help these people? It would be so painful. Wouldn't I rather just put my past life behind me and get on with caring for David and the children? Hadn't I been through enough? The argument in my head continued unabated for some time.

I thought about Chay and the people he'd brought home for me to talk to right at the beginning. I remembered the faith he'd had in me, believing I could tell an alcoholic how to get straight in the time it took him to change his clothes! I thought about the walk he'd been planning and the reason behind it. Chay hadn't been intending to put his past behind him, he'd been planning to use it to help others.

I had a choice to make. As I discussed it with God, I realized that my experience was unique and he was giving me the opportunity to use the years of sadness, to give some meaning to the pain I'd endured. So, instead of leaving my past behind and settling down to domestic bliss with David, I decided I wanted to get up and tell the world about my friend Jesus.

And that's how the walks started, with David's encouragement. Chay's death was a huge loss and in the weeks after he died I found it difficult to even think of the future. But it was David who first reminded me that Chay had planned to walk the coastline of Britain with the large wooden cross he'd made. He wisely suggested that if I did a walk in Chay's place it would be a way of saying 'thank you' to God for his life, for giving him back to me and for the time we'd had together.

Three months after Chay died, therefore, I took up his cross and walked from London to Brighton. It was March

1989, and Chay would have celebrated his eighteenth birthday that month. Chay's intended message was simple: 'If you have a mum or dad who doesn't love you, or who is drinking or neglecting you, I know a man who can help you.' We'd watched him build the cross. It was nine feet six inches tall and six feet six inches wide.

Lindsey Hamon, the man who had originally inspired Chay to walk with a cross, heard about my plans. He knew that David was unwell – although at that stage, several months before our wedding, we weren't aware of the extent of his illness – and offered to walk with me. I was grateful for his company.

We set off on a Saturday and agreed to walk through every park we passed, stop outside every café, talk to every group of people we met – talk, in fact, to anyone who'd listen and tell them Chay's story. I was also going to tell them that I'd been an alcoholic and Jesus had saved my life and given me my son back. I was going to urge people that if they hadn't seen their children for some time or if there was something wrong that they needed to put right, they should go home straight away and sort things out, because tomorrow could be too late.

The first place we stopped at was a pub in the heart of London. We were only five minutes into the walk! I'd never done anything like this before and I was very nervous. As I walked in, all I could see through the smoke haze was a large crowd of men. They were grouped around tables drinking beer and studying the racing papers. I'd obviously walked in at a critical time!

For a moment I thought I'd made a terrible mistake and was tempted to walk straight out again. But I couldn't; I felt as though I was rooted to the spot. So I cleared my throat and shouted, 'Excuse me! I'm walking from London to Brighton and I'd just like to tell you what I'm doing.' I started to tell them my story, but as soon as I said the word 'alcoholic' the barman came over, took hold of my arm, marched me out and firmly shut the door behind me.

Standing outside that pub I was heartbroken. I felt I'd let Jesus down. 'Oh God,' I said, 'I'm so sorry. I've really blown it.'

Straight away I heard the Lord's voice say to me, 'No you haven't, Angie, because you've never been thrown out of a pub sober before!'

That was the best thing he could have said to me. I felt as if he'd put his arms round me and given me a big cuddle. Even though I'd messed up my 'speech', he'd still found something to praise me for, and instead of looking at a defeat I was looking at a win. To me it was certainly a victory to go into a pub and not crave a drink.

I turned round and walked straight back into that pub. 'Excuse me!' I shouted again. 'I really do have something to say to you. You need to listen to me. I'm going to take one minute of your life. Please will you hear me?'

Somebody took my hat off – I was wearing Chay's trilby – and passed it round the pub. Immediately these men were reaching into their pockets and donating coins and £5 notes. 'No please,' I said, 'I'm not collecting money. What I want to tell you is free.' But the hat kept going round and they kept putting money in.

A man who was sitting at a table near where I was standing looked up from his paper and shouted out, 'All right then darlin', tell us what you want to say.' Now the punters had asked me what I wanted to say, so there was nothing the landlord could do to stop me.

Without wasting any more time, I seized my opportunity and promptly told them Chay's story – how he'd grown up without me because of what I'd done over the years; how he came to find me and forgave me; and about the love and forgiveness God had shown to me.

As I was talking, the man who'd invited me to speak started to weep. I stopped and looked at him. 'I haven't seen my children for years,' he said. He described how his wife had left him because of his drinking habit.

Then the man next to him started weeping too. 'I used to get drunk and beat my wife,' he said. 'I don't blame her, but I haven't seen my kids for ages either.' There were three men around that table and within a few minutes they were all weeping. I didn't know what to do next and started to panic again. I was shouting in my head, my heart and my spirit, saying, 'Oh Lord, I don't know what to do now!' God just said to me, 'You can go now, because I am here.'

I knew that what had happened to me that day on the bench, when Jesus came and found me in my alcoholic, homeless state, had just happened to those men. I also knew in my heart that their families were going to see the benefit. The healing process had started for them.

At that point I understood clearly what it was that God was leading me to do for the rest of my life. Visiting that pub was the start of my work in prayer walking for the restoration of family life in this country. In those three men God had shown me the power of my testimony. All I had to do was tell my story – he would do the rest. He'd healed my broken life, even given me another family, and what he'd done for me he would do for anybody.

My one disappointment was that only one person actually gave their life to Christ as a result of that first walk. It seemed an awful lot of effort just for one person. But two years later I did a second walk from London to Brighton. In all I walked 98 miles and 98 people gave their lives to Christ: the Lord gave me one a mile! So the effort I'd put into the first walk was rewarded on the second. I also kept meeting people who remembered me from the first walk, and this time they were keen to approach me to ask what I was doing.

David had been quite right. The therapeutic effect of being able to talk about Chay and see how our story touched the lives of so many people encouraged me to think about the future once more. I'd achieved something worthwhile. By now I'd told my story to hundreds of people. Many had wept, not for me, but for themselves and their own broken families.

I'd held the hands of those sleeping rough. I'd looked into the eyes of alcoholics. I'd hugged children whose mothers were in prison. God had been absolutely right. I could understand their suffering. I told them all about my friend Jesus and how he could help them too.

With two walks under my belt, the question now was not about whether to hang up my walking boots, but about what God wanted me to do next.

eIGHTEEN

Walking for God

By 1992 David was feeling much better. The cancer was in remission, and we discussed the possibility of me undertaking another walk. It was during my second walk from London to Brighton that I was given a clue about my future. It surprised me greatly. I received a message – a prophecy – describing another prayer walk! On the day I was handed this message I was actually feeling quite discouraged. I'd been walking for four days and had hardly talked to anybody. It was pouring with rain and I was trudging across the South Downs, struggling to pull the cross behind me and wondering if I'd made a big mistake.

I was beginning to doubt the value of what I was doing, and was on the point of calling a halt to the walk and going home when a car drew up alongside me. I hadn't heard it approaching. I was so absorbed in my thoughts and the only noise I was aware of was the relentless sound of the howling wind, coupled with the rain lashing against my face.

The driver lowered her window and beckoned to me. I thought she'd probably lost her way and wanted directions. So I was astounded when she said she had a message for me from two women called Judith and Ann. I was even more amazed when she told me the message was actually a prophecy from God saying, 'It would be the sight of the cross going through the land that would bring reconciliation and revival to our nation.'

When I heard these words my spirit jumped, as though I'd been given a gentle kick on the inside. I didn't know what was about to happen, but I believed God had just said something very important and very encouraging to me.

The message delivered, the driver left and I was alone again with my thoughts. It was still raining and there weren't many people about. But I didn't give up. I kept walking that day and decided to pray about this strange incident, asking God to tell me what these words meant and what he wanted me to do.

Thankfully, the next day was fine. After an early breakfast, I started walking again. I hadn't gone far before I started meeting dozens of people. I stopped to chat with each group because they were curious to know why I was walking with a cross. As a result of telling my story that day, 98 people came to Christ. It seemed to me that God had given me a special present and said, 'There you are, that's just a small example of what's going to happen in the future.'

Little did I realize it at the time, but a bit later in that walk I was to encounter somebody who affected my thinking profoundly, and who taught me an important lesson about how to pray effectively for the people and families I was meeting.

I was walking along Telscombe Cliffs, between Newhaven and Brighton. On the cliff path ahead of me I saw a lady walking towards me with a boy and girl on each side of her, who looked to be in their early teens. The three of them had linked arms and seemed to be supporting each other. As we came nearer I thought I heard the Lord say, 'I want you to go and pray for her because her husband died last night.'

Immediately I tried to talk myself out of it. 'I can't say that. What if I'm wrong?' I started to panic, but each step was bringing us closer. The words kept coming to me: 'Her husband died last night. Go over and tell her – I know your husband died last night and the Lord says he loves you.'

I'm ashamed to say that I didn't have the courage to say those exact words, but as this lady came nearer to me I did go over to her. My heart was in my boots. 'Excuse me,' I said nervously, 'can I pray for you?'

As soon as I'd uttered those words, I knew I hadn't said what I believed God had wanted me to say. But the lady turned round and looked at me and put her hand on mine. 'No, dear,' she said, 'you don't need to pray for me. You've done more than you know, because my husband died last night and I came out for a walk begging God to show me he really is there. Thank you for showing me he is real. I saw you coming round the corner with the cross and I knew my prayer had been answered.'

How I wished I'd said the words God had given me! But he didn't reprimand me; he used that experience to teach me that, if I was prepared to listen to him, he'd give me just the right words to say. Meeting that widow taught me that I didn't need to worry about doing or saying anything special – God would tell me what to say! I just had to walk when and where God directed me and let him bring the people across my path that he wanted me to talk to.

After we parted and I carried on walking, I asked myself the question: had God used something to trigger my thinking regarding that woman, or had he spoken to me out of the blue? How did I know her husband had died? Then I realized that what I'd seen was similar to the experience Jesus had when he met the woman at the well.

He understood that because she was there on her own she must have been ostracized by the other women in the village. They'd probably gone out together to fetch their water in the morning when it was cool. But she had come on her own in the afternoon. Therefore it was obvious that she was being shunned because she was considered to be an immoral woman. In the culture of the day such behaviour was punished by isolating the woman from the social group she would normally have mixed with.

I reasoned that if Jesus could draw those conclusions by understanding the social customs of his day, there might be something similar I could learn about the experience I'd just had. So I said to the Lord, 'What was it that I recognized?' And then it came to me that it was the teenage children linking arms with their mother. They were holding her close and that's something you don't normally see these days. You don't even see children of eight or nine hanging onto their mother's arms – it's not cool, not the sort of thing you want your friends to see you doing!

Then I thought how sad it was that it was so rare to see such closeness in a family. God used that to impress into my heart again, even more keenly, the desire to prayer walk for the strengthening of family life in this country, for marriage to be more widely respected, and for children who have lost their fathers. But I had to wait a long time before I found out exactly what the Lord wanted me to do next.

Four years after that second London to Brighton walk, the Lord spoke to me again about my next walk (which came to be known as the Deborah Walk). I hadn't forgotten the message passed to me by the driver of the car that wet day on the South Downs. I hadn't spoken publicly about that bizarre rendezvous, or about the words of the prophecy, but strangely enough, during this time several other people had given me words of encouragement and verses of Scripture. I'd put them in a safe place and they'd helped to keep the idea alive in my heart and mind – but they didn't fully answer my question. I still didn't know exactly what it was God wanted me to do. All I knew was that it was going to be something big. I had a feeling it was going to be something that would sound impossible!

Then it happened. I was woken up at three o'clock one morning by the sound of a choir singing 'Awake awake, oh Deborah', over and over again. As I lay there listening to this chorus of voices I suddenly knew that this had something to do with the prophecy, '...the sight of the cross going through the land that would bring reconciliation and revival to our nation'.

I got up and, taking my Bible with me, crept quietly into the sitting room. I started to read the Old Testament book of Judges, chapters four and five. As I read the story of Deborah, I said to the Lord, 'Just tell me what it is you want me to do.'

Then I began to understand that what I was reading about applied to our society today. The people in the Bible story thought they had everything they needed and were indifferent to God. But in reality their plight was very serious. So God chose a woman, Deborah, a judge and a prophetess, to rescue the people. I was staggered to read that there was a war to fight, and although there were 40,000 men capable of fighting, they didn't have a sword or shield between them; what apathy!

God chose Deborah for the task of leading these men into battle, and in no time at all she had 10,000 soldiers armed and ready for war. I think God gave her the gift of inspiration, enough to make the people get up and do something to help themselves.

It dawned on me then that this was what God wanted me to do too. I was to carry the cross throughout the country and God was going to put an anointing of inspiration upon the cross and upon me. The sight of the cross would cause people to get up and do something about their situation.

I spent the next few hours on the floor sobbing. This was too big a task for me to do. Who was I? Nobody would listen to me!

As I wept, God showed me the sorrow he felt for fatherless children; the heartbreak he had for a nation whose young people were growing up not knowing that he loved them; and the sadness he felt when he saw our broken families. I can't put into words the depth and range of emotions that were going through my heart.

I heard the Lord say, 'I want you to walk for every broken marriage, for every child growing up without the love of a father. I want you to walk and tell the people your story, and I will begin to answer the prayers of ages past.'

God showed me how sad he felt about our disintegrated society, but I also understood, from my own experience, that it was in that place of brokenness and sorrow that God can reach us. That is the only place where we call out to him for help. I could identify with that.

I remembered the book I'd picked up at the Salvation Army jumble sale. My mind went back to the bench where I'd sat for hours, gazing at the picture of Jesus with the crown of thorns on his head. In my sitting room that night I felt him very close to me again. My friend was going to help me; he didn't expect me to do this job on my own. I felt excited at that. My life had taught me that, no matter what mess I get myself into, if I turn to God he can put things right. The one thing I knew from my own experience is that there is always hope.

The Lord showed me many things that night. As dawn broke I felt him say to me, 'It is out of these broken families I will build my church. Then the homosexual can come into my family and be loved and healed. The rapist and the sexual pervert can come in and be totally forgiven and cleansed. Then the people who have been most hurt will be safe in the arms of my people, the church.'

I saw in my mind's eye that the church should be like a well-built house, able to withstand strong winds and torrential rain. When a traveller walks by on a cold, wet night and glances through the window, he sees a warm fire and delicious food on the table. The door is open and as he stands on the threshold he feels it's somewhere he wants to be, somewhere safe and welcoming. So he's drawn in and sits down by the fire, makes himself at home and begins to enjoy all the benefits and comforts that the house has to offer.

I wept and wept. Then the Lord gave me a second vision. I saw a huge stone shelf holding millions of little bottles. It was almost as though I was watching a film. As I took a closer look at the bottles, I noticed that every one had a name label attached. The bottles were full of tears, the tears of all the people who had wept over our land, and God had saved them all.

As I watched, a hand appeared and took a bottle from the shelf. As the tears in that bottle were poured out, they turned to golden oil. I watched as all the bottles were emptied and poured over our land.

Then the Lord said to me, 'Now go, because it is time for the harvest to be released.' He told me to go and talk to other women around the country and encourage them to pray with me and join me on the next walk.

How can I? I thought. Who am I to talk to anybody? I said to God that night, 'Why would they listen to me, Lord? I'm nobody. I'm not famous. They'll think I'm mad.'

But God said, 'Just do it.'

'Do what?' I asked.

'Go and tell them what I've done for you.' Well, I thought, that wasn't a problem – I could do that. But I was still worried. How was I going to start? Who would I speak to first?

In my nervousness I tried to forget the events of that night. A few days later, however, the phone rang and I was surprised to be invited to go and speak at a small church in Norwich. They'd heard about the two London to Brighton walks and were interested to hear my story. As a result of that meeting I was asked to speak at six other churches in the city, one of them an Elim Pentecostal church.

When I arrived there I was overwhelmed to find that over 300 women had come to hear my story. The word was spreading fast! Many of them were Lydia prayer group leaders – women's prayer groups that meet across the country and pray for issues affecting family life, also undertaking prayer walks themselves. As I spoke that evening something supernatural started to happen. I told them my story and then, tentatively, I told them what I believed God had said to me through the story of Deborah.

They sat so quietly while I spoke, you could have heard a pin drop. I kept going. When I'd finished, in case any of them felt they could identify with what I was saying and would like to join me on the Deborah Walk, I invited people to come and stand with me at the front of the church: together we would pray and ask God to help us. I was hoping that one or two would respond positively. I waited uncertainly for their response.

I didn't wait long. Three hundred women came forward that evening, many asking for prayer. It took a long time to pray with them all. The range of problems that surfaced that night and the testimonies that came afterwards were amazing as God touched their lives. A few days later I received letters from some of those women, describing how they'd gone home that night and their marriage had been healed; others went home to find that husbands who'd previously left them had returned.

A recording was made of my talk and tapes were sent all over the world by the women who'd attended the meeting. I needn't have worried about how I was going to tell thousands of women about the Deborah Walk: God gave those 300 women the same gift of inspiration that Deborah had. I nicknamed it the 'Deborah anointing'! They were so enthusiastic and sent tapes everywhere.

I was soon receiving phone calls from Denmark, Bosnia and Holland, and in all of these countries groups of women promised to pray for the walk and for the strengthening of family life in Great Britain. Over 45,000 women promised to pray with me as I walked. Now I began to see what God was doing. One of the most exciting things was seeing the enthusiasm of these women.

I think God used my story because you can't get much lower than I was, or much more disgusting than I was, when Jesus found me. When I'm asked, 'What do you think God looks like?' I reply, 'I think he's got a lovely face and a lovely smile and arms that go on for ever. And it doesn't matter how deep the hole is that you dig for yourself, because his long arms are quite capable of reaching in

and saying, "Come on, sweetheart, I'm pulling you out."
And when he pulls you out of that hole, he wraps his arms
round and round and round and round you until they
bring you up close to his chest. By this time there's so
much arm wrapped around you that nobody can see you;
you're totally hidden and wrapped in his arms!'

After that evening in Norwich, things went crazy. For
a time I was often speaking at five meetings a day. I just
couldn't believe what God was doing and marvelled
at the prayer support network that was being built.
Many people asked for a tape of my talk, and David and
I found ourselves in our little sitting room copying
tapes, stuffing letters in envelopes and sticking on
hundreds of stamps.

We'd planned that the Deborah Walk would start at
John O'Groats in the north and finish at Land's End
in the south. People started to send money. There was
certainly a lot to pay for. We needed a support vehicle
to carry enough food, clothes and literature for three
months. We worked out that if God gave us a van, we'd
need £1,000 to pay for the petrol to get it from John
O'Groats to Land's End.

Our faith was often tested. Just before the walk was
due to start I still didn't have the petrol money. So I
prayed and asked God to sort out this problem. A couple
of days later, a letter arrived from a gentleman who
wrote, 'You won't remember me...' He went on to say
that he'd been moved by hearing my story at a church
meeting one night and had gone home to see if God
would talk to him as well. He'd asked how he could help
with the Deborah Walk and God had replied, 'Send her
£1,000. She's praying for it at the moment.' The cheque
was enclosed with the letter.

Damian, David's son, offered to join me on the walk, and so did Angela Fairlamb from Guildford. We planned to start the walk on 1 June 1997.

Two weeks prior to the start, David became very ill again. The cancer that had been in remission for six years came back with a vengeance. It looked as though all our plans would have to be scrapped. How could I leave my husband when his life was once more in the balance?

nINETEEN

The Deborah
Walk

David ordered me to walk! He was quite emphatic. He argued that if we gave up before we started, we were admitting defeat. After many days of deliberation we decided that being obedient to God was the only criteria. Experience had taught us that our own reasoning is often flawed because our understanding is limited. We can only see what's in front of us. But God sees the whole picture, so we preferred to trust him and believe that he would look after us all, especially David.

I still felt torn in half. I loved David so much that it hurt me to have to leave him behind. It felt like a very high price to pay. Even at that point I would quite happily have delayed the walk. It took me a few days to reach a position where I could accept that if I was doing what God wanted me to do, he would look after David.

I had only to remember that 45,000 women had promised to pray for the walk to be reminded of the support God had already given me. That gave me great strength. And even though in my heart I wanted to be at home caring for David, I'll always be grateful to him for encouraging me to go ahead. I couldn't have left him otherwise.

David's illness wasn't the only problem we had. The support vehicle that had been promised was not forthcoming. When the time came to start the journey up to Scotland so that we could begin the walk, we still had no van and no driver. David was to have driven us up to Scotland, but it was obvious that he couldn't. Instead we hired a car, which used up a vast amount of the money we'd allocated for petrol for the van.

Despite this setback, Damian, Angela and I were unanimous in believing that God was encouraging us to trust him, to take the first step in faith. From that moment, we believed, he would be the fourth member of the team and would provide everything we needed. It was blind faith and very exciting!

We left London as planned on 1 June 1997 and travelled to Thurso in Scotland, where we stayed the night with John and Marjorie Gunn. It was a curious situation to be in: we were planning to start the walk the next morning and still we had no van and no driver, and the £1,000 we'd allocated for our petrol money had been seriously eroded by the cost of the hire car. To the sceptical onlooker we hardly looked like a group of people who were going to make it to Land's End!

However, the Christian community in Thurso knew we were coming and had been praying. That evening John visited a friend of his called George to ask him if he would be our driver. George, a former soldier and recovering alcoholic, was prepared to volunteer, but he was concerned about how his rent would be paid while he was away. The Christians promised to pay his rent for him and look after his flat in his absence. So that just left the problem of the van.

Later that night, we had a call to say that friends in a nearby village who'd heard about our need a few days earlier thought the ex-hippie bus parked at the bottom of their garden might be suitable. It was 27 years old, but they'd managed to get it working and roadworthy.

An hour later we heard it arrive! The keys were handed to George with an MOT certificate – it had passed the test only that evening! Driver and van were duly introduced. Full of encouragement and amazement at how God had answered our prayers, we loaded up, ready to leave early the next morning.

As I lay awake that night I wondered what lay ahead of us. Hundreds of miles, months of walking. Would we make it? Would David live long enough to see us finish? We set off on the walk the next day not knowing how we'd be able to afford the food for the journey, let alone the fuel. But by the third day we were actually giving away carrier bags full of food from the van, we'd been given so much! And that set the pattern. God provided for us throughout the walk. We were never short of anything for long.

When we set off from John O'Groats a large crowd of people walked with us. Amongst them was an elderly lady in her eighties and she told me about her husband who had Alzheimer's disease. She walked 17 miles with us that first day and as she walked she was praying that God would heal her husband. I found it quite heartbreaking to watch her walking ahead of me carrying the cross on her shoulder, her white hair blowing in the wind.

Towards the end of that first day a car slowly overtook us. It was driven by this lady's son. He parked the car and started walking towards her. Then the passenger door opened – and out got her husband. He walked over to his wife and the two of them embraced. They walked a little way together, carrying the cross. We watched in silence and wept as we witnessed God answering her prayers. And we asked God to forgive us for thinking that he wouldn't bother healing an old man in his eighties.

Of course, there were days when we were tempted to give up. Days when the rain soaked us to the skin and we were numb with cold. In Scotland we battled for mile after mile against the wind until we were exhausted. Some days we didn't meet a soul, but trudged for miles along lonely roads and dual carriageways and grass verges. Walking through the Cairngorms we almost got frostbite (by the time we got as far south as Bristol we were being scorched by the sun). Lorries passing us at great speed made it very difficult even to hold the cross upright. But every day we spurred each other on.

As you would expect, sometimes tiredness caused tension between us and the atmosphere in the group on some days was unpleasant. Then we were glad of the opportunity to stride out and walk alone for a few miles to let the anger and frustration we felt cool down. But every night we prayed together and tried to make it our aim to settle our differences before we went to sleep. It was too exhausting to have bad feeling between us for long.

As we approached each town we wondered what reaction we'd spark off as we walked through with the cross. It wasn't long before people heard we were on the way. By then we'd started to attract quite a lot of media attention. Walking steadily down through Scotland, we planned to walk through Possils Park in Glasgow, a notorious, even dangerous, area of the city well known for its prostitutes, drug dealers and high crime rate.

It was one of the most run-down places I'd ever seen. The doorways stank of urine; many of the shops were boarded up; graffiti covered the walls; litter was strewn everywhere; prostitutes and transvestites were standing in doorways plying their trade; drug addicts and dealers were openly engaging in broad daylight.

A couple of days before we reached the outskirts of Glasgow I'd spoken at a church in Stirling and a reporter from a local newspaper had been there. After the meeting he'd asked if he could take a photograph of me with the cross. I ended up on the front pages of *The Daily Record*, looking rather glamorous with the cross on my shoulder and wearing high-heeled boots because I was dressed for speaking and not for walking!

This caused quite a lot of amusement between us, but it proved useful, because as I walked through the centre of Possils Park a few days afterwards, people recognized me. The headline in the paper had read, 'Ex-Prostitute and Drug Addict Walks for Families' and the story had obviously caught the local people's imagination.

Men climbed down from some scaffolding to come over and speak to us; many other people stopped to watch us pass. We were treated with a lot of respect. As we turned the final corner into Possils Park we saw windows being opened three storeys up. Some women looked down and shouted, 'Ang! Get there for us, darlin'!' These were prostitutes.

'You can do it for yourself!' I shouted back. 'Come on down and we'll tell you how!'

Colin Cuthbert, then head of Christian Prison Ministries, was walking with us. He tapped me on the shoulder and surreptitiously said, 'Look over there.' I looked casually in the direction he'd indicated and saw people who were clearly dealing in drugs. As we walked slowly deeper into Possils Park, we became aware that some people were leaving the dealers and coming over towards us.

We knew we were walking through areas where even the police were wary to go. Gangs there are violent. It was quite likely that we were surrounded by youths carrying knives and guns. Many of them were high on drugs, others were agitated because they needed another fix.

A queue started to form behind us and we stopped and waited as the people came closer. I was praying all the time; my heart went out to these people. Only a few years earlier my life had been like theirs. I walked towards them and started to speak, explaining what I was doing walking with a large wooden cross. I told them my life story and about Chay and how we'd been reunited. I invited them to write their names on the cross if they wanted God to come and help them. One by one they knelt by the cross and wrote their names on it.

We stayed there some time, talking and praying with the people who crowded round. The next morning we listened to the news on the radio and heard that the previous night the police had raided several addresses in Possils Park, confiscating drugs worth over £7 million and arresting several dealers.

We were amazed. It seemed that God was already answering the prayers of those people who'd come to the cross asking for help the day before. Already God had said, 'Yes, I've heard your prayers and now this is what I'll do for you.'

As we started walking that morning, we saw an elderly man outside a shop who looked as though he was waiting for someone. I crossed over the road to ask him if he wanted to put his name on the cross. 'Hi,' I said, 'what's your name?' But he couldn't speak and seemed to be indicating to me that he'd had a stroke. He was really trying to talk, but he just couldn't get the words out.

So I asked him to write his name directly on the cross and offered to pray for him. But he indicated that the stroke had affected the right side of his body and, being right handed, he couldn't write either!

I was starting to run out of ideas and was desperately trying to think of a way of helping this man to communicate, when he suddenly shouted out, 'Robert McCoy!' Well, now he could speak but the rest of us couldn't! We just stood there with our mouths open. We hadn't even prayed for him. All we'd done was go over to him with the cross, and God had healed him there and then. I cried. He cried. The whole team cried for Robert McCoy!

We also met Andy that day. I saw him walking along the road clutching a carrier bag – or what I call a 'take-away'. In alcoholic circles that's another name for the bag in which you carry your drink for the day. He was quite smartly dressed, and obviously hadn't got to the stage where he was neglecting to look after himself, so I presumed he was probably a 'top-up' drinker, someone who's always drunk.

As we got closer he looked me straight in the eye and said, 'I was expecting you. I knew you would come.'

'Did you?' I replied, slightly unnerved by his penetrating stare.

'I knew you would come. Oh God, I've been expecting you for such a long time.'

I asked him his name and he told me he was called Andy. I talked to him about his drinking, which he denied at first. Then I invited him to write his name on the cross and he responded positively and seemed pleased to be asked. But as he approached the cross he jumped back and was very afraid. So I asked him if he'd like us to pray with him first, then he could try again to write his name on the cross.

We prayed and he tried again. He stepped forward, but he couldn't come close enough to the cross. I reached out my hand, touched his forehead and said, 'Come Holy Spirit.' Then I prayed for him again.

All of a sudden he put his arms round my neck and just sank to his knees. This was all happening in the middle of the road! So there we were, on our knees with the cross balanced over the two of us. The team were standing nearby.

Andy started to cry. 'Oh, thank you for making me cry, thank you for making me cry, oh God, thank you for making me cry,' he wept. We must have knelt there for about 20 minutes and I held him until he'd stopped sobbing. Then he looked up at me and I gave him the pen and he wrote his name on the cross.

We took him onto the pavement after that and prayed with him again before we walked on. 'Oh, please don't go, please don't go!' he pleaded with us. It broke my heart, but we had to go on. We couldn't stay: there were more people like Andy to meet. We left him sitting on a bench.

As we turned the corner we bumped into a person called Liz, who'd joined us on the walk the previous day. She was with a friend, an ex-alcoholic who was now a Christian. So we were able to tell them about Andy and they went round the corner straight away to pick up where we'd left off. Everything was under control; God had it all worked out. I couldn't resist a final look back at Andy. As I peered round the corner after Liz and her friend, I saw that she had her arm around Andy and they were already talking together.

We stayed with Liz and her husband that night and set off again early the next morning after a huge breakfast. We walked all day and were just considering where we were going to stop for the night when we received an urgent message on our mobile phone. 'Please could you come back. Liz's husband has been taken seriously ill.' He'd been suffering from ME for some time. We turned the van round at once and retraced our steps.

We prayed with Liz and her husband that night before leaving again the next morning. We didn't hear anything for two or three days, as we were walking through a remote part of Scotland. Then, out of the silence, we heard a driver beeping his horn. A car pulled up just ahead of us and out got Liz and her husband. He walked seven miles with us that day! Once again our prayers had been answered.

As news travelled ahead of us and people heard we were on the way, we received many requests from churches to visit their towns or villages. I think I'd still be walking today if I'd accepted every invitation we were offered! These invitations could be very compelling – 'Please come and pray with us, you have no idea how bad things are in our neighbourhood.'

I quickly had to learn an important lesson: nothing *I* did would change those people's circumstances. Only God moving amongst them could make the difference. My responsibility was to keep my own life clean and be obedient to what God was asking me to do. I soon realized that flattery is very beguiling.

We were becoming very tired from walking all day and speaking in churches at night. There were always so many people to pray for and it was not uncommon for us to crawl into our sleeping bags at one or two in the morning and be up walking by seven.

One night I put the map on the ground and asked God about all these requests, and he showed me that he would lead me to the people who really were in darkness. They were the voiceless folk and he wanted us to take his message of love and hope to them. All we had to remember was that we were walking with Jesus by our side.

We were to pray for the schools we passed, that the word of God would be taught properly. We were to pray for every church we passed, that it would be respected and effective in its community. After that we were to pray carefully about our route and always agree together on the right way forward.

We were well aware that we were walking through some areas where there had been a history of abuse, and where terrible things had allegedly happened in the past – places where blood had been shed, and even satanic rituals carried on year after year, generation after generation. But Jesus encouraged us to pray that we would quite simply stay close to him, so that he could take us to the people he wanted to touch. That comforted us – it felt so manageable!

We noticed that people's reactions to God changed when they saw we weren't judging them, but rather loving them and telling them about how Jesus had helped us. When we did that, we noticed that people judged themselves: we didn't have to say a word.

tWENTY

All the difference in the world

We reached Land's End on Wednesday 27 August 1997. It had taken us 86 days to walk 1,098 miles.

I have memories from the Deborah Walk that will stay with me for the rest of my life. I took my black German Shepherd called Shadow on the walk and, until he became too footsore, he was a valuable member of the team. It soon became apparent that he had his own unique role to play. Only he could communicate with the people we met who wouldn't talk directly to us, because they'd been so badly hurt by people and only trusted animals.

One day, while we were walking through a wild, sparsely populated region in Scotland, we came across a little shop in the middle of a small hamlet. We'd walked many miles that day and had met nobody, so we were looking forward to chatting with the shopkeeper. Our driver, George, had arrived in the village ahead of us as usual and was sitting in the van waiting for us to join him.

'The woman who runs that shop really hates God,' he told us, 'but she loves animals.' He'd spoken to her earlier, when he'd called to buy a few provisions. She'd seen our bus, which was somewhat conspicuous as it had a sign on the side saying 'The Premier Deborah Walk'

(Premier Radio covered our walk in a series of weekly bulletins) and another sign saying 'Jesus loves you'. George had told her the story and the reason behind the walk, but her initial reaction had been hostile, and she admitted she had no time for God, even hated him.

'Oh does she,' I said. George smiled knowingly at me. 'Shall I take Shadow in to meet her?'

'Yes,' he said. 'I've told her all about him.'

Shadow is an exuberant dog, very large and extremely friendly. I kept him on a short lead and told him to be on his best behaviour as we slowly walked over to the shop. As I opened the door I saw the shopkeeper watching me from behind the counter.

'My driver has told me you like animals, so I thought you'd like to meet my dog,' I said, smiling at her.

She looked at me in silence for a moment, her eyes betraying the distrust she felt towards me. Shadow started to wag his tail, perhaps sensing the tension between us. Alsatians are intelligent dogs and quick to assess the mood of the people they're with. He knew this woman couldn't resist him! And he was right. She looked at Shadow, his big, brown, sensitive eyes stared straight into hers, and she came out from behind the counter and made a great fuss of him.

Still stroking Shadow and looking at him rather than me, she said, 'Don't talk to me about God. You didn't see my seven-year-old daughter when she died. She died of Leukaemia and she died in agony, and I don't want to know about a God who kills children like that.' Tears came to her eyes as she continued, 'I have my 13 dogs and that's all I need.'

'You've got 13 dogs?' I said, impressed. She told me they were all Dobermans, and they were her only family. She'd obviously experienced deep loss and unhappiness and had retreated to live alone in this remote part of Scotland. She went on to tell Shadow all about her dogs and he listened patiently.

As she told him how much they loved her, and he responded by licking her face and whining with delight, I was desperately trying to think what I could say to her that might help. Then God said to me, 'Tell her she's spelt my name backwards 13 times.'

I waited for a few more seconds, before quietly saying what God had told me to. I'd learned to do that by then, however awkward or odd it might seem. As soon as I'd finished saying the words, that lady rested her head against Shadow's and started to cry uncontrollably. A few minutes later, as we talked, she came to understand and accept that God loved her.

The Deborah Walk didn't take the most direct route from John O'Groats to Land's End. We decided to walk through Wales as well. It was there that I met a couple called Cathy and Paul, another story which stands out in my memory among so many others. I'd been invited to speak one evening to a large crowd of people in a church in mid-Wales.

During the meeting the Lord gave me a message and told me it was for two people, a young man on one side of the room and a young woman on the opposite side. I explained to the meeting what I believed God wanted to say to this couple. And as if that wasn't enough, I pointed to the two people I believed God had shown me were to receive the message.

Everybody started to laugh and I asked what was so funny. The message had seemed quite serious to me. The two young people stood up and said that although they were married, they'd been been living apart for a while and were considering divorce. That word from God brought them back together and that same night they were reunited with their five children, who meanwhile had been cared for by their grandmother.

I didn't expect to see Cathy and Paul again, but when I reached Land's End, at the end of the walk, they were there to meet me. They'd travelled all the way from Wales because they wanted us to baptize them in the sea. They were so grateful to God for healing their marriage and they publicly wanted to dedicate the rest of their lives to working for him. I thought that was a wonderful ending to the Deborah Walk. Their story somehow typified the reason why we'd walked all that way, and I was very moved.

David was at Land's End to meet me. I had previously discussed with him how I wanted the walk to end. With only a few yards to go before we crossed the finishing line, David walked towards me. I felt so proud of him. I placed the cross on his shoulder and we walked together to the end of the road. David had walked every step of the way with me in his spirit. He was as much part of the walk as any of us, and as my husband and the head of our family I felt it was significant that he was with me that day and we were seen to be the team we undoubtedly are.

Other friends had also journeyed to Land's End to meet us. There was quite a crowd, many of whom I hadn't seen for nearly three months. We all processed down the road towards the sea to baptize Cathy and Paul, and we saw that there was a festival going on. Hundreds of New Age travellers were there, and bikers too – in fact the whole cove was packed with these people.

We got ready to go into the sea for the baptism and it wasn't long before we noticed that we'd created quite a lot of interest. Many of the festival-goers came down onto the beach to watch what was going on. One young man started to heckle us. 'Well,' he said scornfully, 'tell me why you think there's only one God. What about all the people on the other planets? Don't you think they have gods too?'

He bombarded us with questions for over half an hour. Some were quite shocking and sordid, and it was obvious that he was under the influence of drugs and very anti-Christ. But he drew an audience and each time we answered him he'd come back with a counter-argument.

Eventually we went down into the sea and baptized Cathy and Paul, but as soon as we came out of the water this young man resumed his attack. He started to shout even more loudly at us and a young woman whom he obviously knew joined in with him in a jeering sort of way.

This young woman had three children with her and was sitting in a car. She appeared to be very angry, but the Lord said to me that she was only angry because her boyfriend had spent the money she'd saved for the children's tea on alcohol. So she was angry. She was sad. She felt let down. She was just giving vent to her feelings. What could I do to help her and show her that God loved her?

We had a little money left in the van from what we'd been given to help us buy food and petrol for our journey. God reminded me of this and I ran back to our van to fetch it. Then I went over to the young woman and put the money into her hand. Holding her hands in mine, I looked into her eyes and said, 'This is for your children's tea.' She immediately started to cry and I said, 'Jesus told me to give it to you.' With that I walked quietly away. I don't know what happened to her afterwards; I didn't even find out her name. Maybe I'll meet her again one day, maybe I won't, but I know she met Jesus that day.

Chay had inspired the Deborah Walk, but it was Bonita I had been praying for as every mile passed. I ached to be reconciled with my daughter and it was my prayer that she would be at Land's End to meet me. I'd dreamed of seeing her again, of holding her and telling her how sorry I was for the unhappiness I'd caused her. I searched for her face in the crowd. Surely she would be there. But it wasn't to be. I had to wait a few more months before we could be reunited again.

It's strange how history repeats itself. One day the phone rang and it was my sister Pam to say that Bonita was at her house and wanted to meet me. Six months after I returned home from the walk, there she was. She told me she was planning to get married. Together we planned the wedding, and I made her wedding dress and gave her away. What an honour after all those years.

I'm often asked what the Deborah Walk achieved. I suppose the truthful answer to that is, 'I don't fully know.' But what I do know is that hundreds of marriages were mended. I have letters from scores of people telling me their stories.

I'm also often asked to describe the most useful lesson I've learnt in life. My answer is simple, but I've tested it well and proved it to be true: if the light of the world is living in me, I can make a difference to every life I pass. When I stand in darkness, or darkness threatens to surround and engulf me, I just declare that I am a child of God, living in his light.

I know what darkness is. I know what despair is like. But I also know that it only takes one small candle to light a dark room. Its flame can be seen from a great distance. And as I've walked closer to the brightest light I know, the darkness in my own life has disappeared. God has made all the difference in the world to me.

Today, David is still fighting cancer. I've just been diagnosed as having rheumatoid arthritis. My hair has fallen
out and I'm in constant pain. But nothing can deflect me
from my walk with God. It will continue, come what may.
I'm already planning my next prayer walk – in China.

To Jesus

I don't know what You see in me
You who died for humanity
why You left the hundred to look for me
why You cared enough to set me free.

For I'm just a worthless whore.

But You cut the chains that bound me
and taught me only a slave is free.
You gave me back my dignity
and opened the door to eternity.

For me, a worthless whore.

You are the one who lifted me
out of a life of debauchery.
You clothed me in a robe of sanctity
and still You keep forgiving me.

Me, a worthless whore.

So who am I who writes I'm free,
saved from a life of heresy,
in love with Him who first loved me?
I'm the worthless whore mentioned here, You see,

and Angie is my name.

Postscript

Angie's husband, David, has the last word...

It has been said, although I don't remember by whom, that a man is rarely a hero to his wife. Whatever the truth of this, I'm able to say with complete conviction that my wife is a heroine to me.

I'm not speaking of her long walks carrying a large cross, although there's much of the heroic about those. She's had her life threatened by satanists and militant feminists and, on a walk in Ireland, shared the gospel of peace with armed terrorists. She's walked on despite huge blisters, a bruised shoulder, cold, drizzle and hunger. She's rallied her team with determination when most wanted to pack up and go home.

But there are other reasons why Angie is a heroine to me. Probably only a husband would know about the pain she relives daily in the telling of her testimony. She delights in the way God uses her painful story to reach out to others, but it isn't without cost. I've lost count of how often she's said that she doesn't want to go on sharing her life publicly, that she wants to give it all up and just be my wife. But whenever the Master calls, she responds.

That call may take her to a pulpit, a stage or a television studio. More often she'll find herself face to face with another broken woman whose past has overtaken her present, and who needs the touch of Jesus, who suffers with them both. It is then that Angie has to turn back once again and reach down into the agony of her own past.

Now that is heroism.

We want to hear from you. Please send your comments about this
book to us in care of the address below. Thank you.

GRAND RAPIDS, MICHIGAN 49530 USA

WWW.ZONDERVAN.COM